THE
CONWY VALLEY
LINE

BLAENAU FFESTINIOG to LLANDUDNO JUNCTION

1.Blaenau Ffestiniog. c. 1932

G. H. Platt

COMPILED and WRITTEN by

BILL REAR

ACKNOWLEDGEMENTS

This work has once again depended heavily on the generous assistance given so freely by many good friends, who supplied information and photographs from their collections. Particular thanks must be extended to the following who supplied photographs:D.H. Ballantyne, Peter Baughan, British Rail, London Midland Region, C.L.Caddy, W.A.Camwell, Colin Cartwright, of the Conwy Valley Museum, H.C. Casserley, Derek Chaplin, D.J. Clarke, R.H. Clarke, Clwyd Record Office, Brian Cowlishaw, David Cross, J.J. Davis, Larry Goddard, Gwynedd Record Office, Vernon Griffiths, Mrs Maud House, Norman Jones, Norman Kneale, Michael Mensing,Joe Moss, Mrs Kathleen Platt, for access to the work of her late husband Geoff. H. Platt, Alan Pratt, H.B. Priestley, H. Rogers Jones, E.S. Russell, Dave Southern and D. Thompson. Thanks also to Bob Dennis, Vic Roberts of British Rail Chester, Gordon Griffiths and Andy Jones, Llandudno Junction, Mr Merrick Roocroft of Chester, whose co-operation with on-going research is much appreciated. To Bill Lynn of Low Fell, Derek Foster of Kirkby, Henry and Janet Wilson of Tarvin. Especial thanks to John Kimberley and Gareth Haulfryn Williams for assistance and support in the research, Eddie Johnson for photographic work, and my publishers Greg and Jacqueline Fox, for their continued support. Finally to my wife Norma, without whose co-operation, help and tolerance this work could not have been made.

Bill Rear.
JOHNSTOWN, Wrexham.

This work is dedicated to men and women of Llandudno Junction shed and in particular to two drivers, Bill Griffiths and Tom Gill, with fond memories of their guidance and tuition.

Designed and edited by Gregory K. Fox
Typeset by Bill Rear, Johnstown, Wrexham, Clwyd.
Printed by The Amadeus Press, Huddersfield.

Published by Foxline Publishing.
32 Urwick Road, Romiley, Stockport. SK6 3JS

2. Blaenau Ffestiniog. 1904.

Photo: Vernon Griffiths

THE CONWY VALLEY LINE
BLAENAU FFESTINIOG to LLANDUDNO JUNCTION

Historical

The Conwy Valley line extends from Llandudno Junction, on the North Wales coast, to the original terminus at Blaenau Ffestiniog, a distance of 27 miles. This excludes, of course the extension of the line to the 1982 station on the site of the former GW branch terminus, and beyond, to Trawsfynydd, on the former Bala and Ffestiniog line. One of the early proposals for the branch, about 1846, was to leave the coast line under the castle walls at Conwy and follow the Gyffyn valley to Llanrwst via Dolgarrog and Trefriw. Subsequently, in 1853, a proposal was put forward by the Conway & Llanrwst Railway to build a line along the east bank of the river but this was withdrawn in favour of a stated Chester & Holyhead (C.& H.) preferred route along the west bank. In 1858 however, a proposal was made by Edmund Sharpe of Lancaster for a narrow gauge line 3' 3" gauge, to Llanrwst, along the west side of the valley, but despite receiving a sympathetic hearing by '*The Railway Times*', the project was dismissed by the C.& H.R. at a meeting in September 1858. Ultimately, the Conway and Llanrwst Railway received its Royal Assent on 23rd July 1860 and the first sod was cut on 25th August of the same year, at Llanrwst Abbey. However, two months later, the L.N.W.R. resolved to buy the necessary land with their own Hedworth Lee being appointed as engineer. Subsequently the C.& H. itself became absorbed by the L.N.W.R., confirmed by Act of 1863.

This $11\frac{1}{4}$ miles of line was single throughout, with sidings at Llanrwst and intermediate stations at Llansaintffraid (subsequently re-named Glan Conway), and Tal-y-Cafn. Connection with the main line was effected at Llandudno Junction with the branch line trains having their own separate line and platform. The line was inspected by Captain Rich on 9th June 1863, with opening subject to the provision of an engine turntable at Llanrwst within six weeks. One week later, a special inaugural train left Llandudno for Llanrwst with all the usual ceremony that befitted such an important event in rural communities. Public services started the following day. The railway premises at Llanrwst comprised a passenger station, goods station and yard, and an engine shed, all of which were constructed by J.Gibson & Son for the sum of £3,161. In 1881 the engine shed and old tank-house were demolished and the materials used in the rebuilding of Holyhead Shed boundary wall. The 42ft turntable here was also removed and installed at Llanberis, where it remained out of use from the 1920s until the late 1950s.

From the outset, the picturesque scenery of the line was exploited, as were the mineral waters of Llanrwst. There was some competition from river steamers which worked upstream to the coast, and variations on the river traffic survived until the outbreak of World War 2. The initial train service consisted of three trains each way, a number which was increased to five by June 1864.

3. Blaenau Ffestiniog. 24th September 1904. The station in its hey day. The nest of wagons in the tranship siding include the special narrow gauge transporter wagons, the sixth vehicle of which awaits unloading. Two narrow gauge Gunpowder wagons stand apart on the siding adjacent to the goods shed. A train of six wheel coaches for Llandudno awaits at the platform, beyond which is the carriage and loco shed in the background.

British Railways L.M. Region

The L.N.W.R. was authorised to extend the railway to Betws y Coed by an Act of 5th July 1865 and so the $3^3/_4$ miles extension left the Conway & Llanrwst formation north of Llanrwst old station - which was replaced by a new building south of the junction - the line being opened for goods traffic on 18th October 1867. At Betws, sidings were provided, with slate earning much revenue for the line. Passenger services commenced on 6th April 1868 and the station refreshment rooms opened the same summer. A service of five trains daily worked to and from Betws y Coed on week days. A single road stone locomotive shed was built on the Up side north of the station, but there are no reports of it being used for that purpose at any time. During the 1914-18 war it was used as a road vehicle store, according to the late Bill Griffiths of Llandudno Junction shed, who started work at Betws y Coed about that time. The structure survived until shortly before World War 2 when it was demolished, although the water tank, column, and inspection pit between the tracks survived until the loop was removed.

During the construction of the Betws extension the quarry owners at Blaenau Ffestiniog made approaches to the L.N.W.R. with a view to extending their line to the quarries, because of difficulties encountered with the Festiniog Railway, an undertaking still using horse power and the consequent delay in moving their products. As a result, the L.N.W.R. surveyed various routes, but the unescapable fact of a long tunnel to reach Blaenau caused the Company to consider both narrow (1' $11^5/_8$") and standard gauges for an acceptable route, via the Lledr or Penmachno valleys. Due to financial problems, progress was halted on this proposal for a time, during which the Festiniog Railway introduced steam power, the improvement in traffic to the Slate Quarry owners resulting in their refusal to guarantee business to the L.N.W.R. The narrow gauge proposals were thus revived by the L.N.W.R. in 1870, using the Lledr valley route. Although the original proposal to effect a junction with the Festiniog Railway was withdrawn from the L.N.W.R. Bill a new narrow gauge line was surveyed, south and east of the former scheme, terminating at a junction with the Festiniog Railway's Dinas branch. A new 'Betws and Ffestiniog', line which specified gauges of 1' $11^5/_8$" or wider, but not to exceed standard, received the Royal Assent on 18th July 1872.

By August of the same year, the decision was taken to bore out the long tunnel beneath Moel Dyrnogydd to standard gauge. Unfortunately, tenders for its construction exceeded those estimates so much that the L.N.W.R. instructed their recently appointed engineer to the Chester and Holyhead District, William Smith, to do the work. Work had commenced on the narrow gauge, but by May 1873 however, it was realised that despite the advanced state of the works, it would be necessary for the L.N.W.R. to construct special locomotives and rolling stock to work this line, so the decision was taken to reconstruct to standard gauge, which involved a number of alterations having to be made to the curves, earthworks and bridges. Hand boring of the tunnel started in January 1874, and so the Betws Extension Railway was authorised, which continued the new line for nearly one mile to a new terminus near Blaenau market hall. By January 1878, single platform stations at Roman Bridge and Pont-y-pant were put to contract, and a loop with island platform at Dolwyddelan was authorised. Colonel Rich inspected alterations and improvements to Llanrwst and Tal-y-Cafn where second platforms and passing loops had been installed, although Betws still had only one platform. The Colonel demanded that if trains were to cross

at this point, there should be two, but this was ignored by the L.N.W.R.

The line to Dolwyddelan was in use for local freight by February 1879, and at Blaenau, a temporary station was erected immediately south of the tunnel mouth in order that the line might open for traffic whilst the Betws Extension Railway was completed. The $11^1/_2$ mile line was inspected by Colonel Rich in June 1879, who tested the width of the single line 3726 yard tunnel by walking in front of a locomotive propelling a carriage at walking speed, with doors open on both sides, from end to end. The summit of the line is reached inside the tunnel, about $^1/_4$ mile from the Ffestiniog end. There were four other tunnels of short length on the line. The Lledr viaduct, with seven stone arches, is the other major feature, with seventeen bridges of lesser size constructed mainly of large undressed stone, a detail with which the Colonel found fault. After a re-inspection, the railway between Betws y Coed and the temporary station at Blaenau was opened on 22nd July 1879, the extension to the permanent station opening on 1st April 1881, after which the temporary station was closed and removed. At Blaenau, a combined locomotive and carriage shed was built which contained one and three roads respectively for each section. The shed was closed on 14th September 1931 and afterwards demolished. The L.N.W.R. opened the 'North Western Hotel' adjoining the station at Blaenau in 1881, but the venture failed to live up to expectations, and consequently was let off privately and sold in 1906.

The original junction with the Chester and Holyhead line of the L.N.W.R. was almost opposite the junction of the Llandudno branch and at the point where the first Llandudno Junction station stood. The line, which was single throughout, followed close along the shore between the engine shed and the water line. The present Llandudno Junction station was opened on 1st October 1897 when the first station was closed and demolished. The branch junction was moved further east and half a mile of new line was built. The original branch line was retained as a long siding, although the last hundred yards towards Glan Conway was taken up, becoming part of the motive power department and being used to store locomotives out of traffic during the winter months.

The line was controlled by block working from 1879, a system replaced in 1894 by electric staff, coincidental with the signal box at Dolwyddelan being replaced by a frame mounted on the island platform. In July 1898, the goods loop on the Down side at Betws y Coed became the Down Passenger line with the introduction of a new platform, reached by a footbridge. The Up line was signalled for Up and Down line working by the L.N.W.R. in contravention of the Board of Trade requirements, although an exception was permitted for trains that terminated at Betws and worked back to Llandudno Junction.

In 1908, the 'Abbey, Dolgarrog & Trefriw Light Railway was approved and confirmed by the Dolgarrog Light Railway Order of 1910. This was built as a Government Work during World War I from the Ffestiniog branch to the aluminium works at Dolgarrog, and which crossed the river. A new halt, with the name of 'Dolgarrog' came into use in 1917. In 1912, a standard gauge light railway entitled 'The Conway Valley Light Railway' to run on the west side of the Conwy was approved but came to nothing.

The scenery along the line was recognised as a major tourist attraction from the outset and was publicised from early days to encourage holiday traffic to the area. In September 1911 the L.N.W.R. introduced a third class 'Observation' car on the morning Down journey to Blaenau, returning in the afternoon, with a supplementary fare for passengers. This facility was increased when two more cars were built in 1913, and proved extremely popular. They were used on this seasonal basis continuously until the outbreak of World War 2 when they were withdrawn for the duration. Reinstatement after hostilities continued every summer season until the introduction of the Lightweight D.M.U.s in 1956 when the large panoramic windows of the units rendered the steam hauled stock surplus to requirements on the line. The observation cars were also used daily on the Llanberis excursion traffic that ran Mondays to Fridays from Prestatyn and Rhyl until the end of excursion services on that line

Description of the Line

The branch leaves the Chester and Holyhead main line on the Down side and turns through ninety degrees to run alongside the river Conwy. The first station, originally called Llansaintffraid but renamed Glan Conway in 1865, was $1\frac{1}{2}$ miles from the Junction, and the single low platform was located on the Down side, the line being built on a sea wall. Due to the difficulty in getting land, no goods accommodation was provided but there was a small siding, controlled by the train staff, also on the Down side and south of the station. During the summer months after World War 2, a camping coach was located here. The station closed in December 1964 but reopened in 1971. The siding was removed in 1965. The line closely followed the river - which is tidal up to the quay at Trefriw - to the first crossing loop $5\frac{1}{4}$ miles from the Junction, at Tal-y-Cafn & Eglwysbach, a station which had a loop and two platforms. Public access between platforms was across a walkway, and a road level crossing, protected by hand operated gates, were at the south end of the station. Beyond the crossing on the Down side was a small goods yard. As previously mentioned another wooden platform halt was built at Dolgarrog ($8\frac{1}{4}$ miles) on the Down side, opened in 1917 to serve the Aluminium works across the river. Just before the platform was a siding on the Up side, with a connection to the private branch line which crossed the river and led to the Hydro-electric station and Aluminium works. Between Dolgarrog and Llanrwst were two sidings; the Abbey sidings at 9 miles on the Down side, and Cae Coch siding at $9\frac{1}{2}$ miles on the Up side, both closing before World War 2. At $10\frac{1}{2}$ miles was Tan Lan siding on the Down side, immediately followed by Llanrwst signal box on the Up side. At this point, the extension to Betws y Coed diverged on the Down side from the Conway and Llanrwst Railway, which continued straight on for about 200 yards to the original terminal station in Llanrwst goods yard.

The Betws y Coed line then reached the present Llanrwst North station, originally Llanrwst & Trefriw, until the construction of the new Llanrwst platform in 1990. Llanrwst North consists of a passing loop and two platforms, the main buildings being on the Up side. Passengers crossed the line by an open footbridge numbered 6A. The goods yard was extremely busy until traffic was diverted to road in the mid 1960s. Half a mile beyond the station is a short tunnel, 85 yards in length, under a portion of the town. The new Llanrwst station platform is located on the Down side just south of the tunnel.

The line continues to follow the course of the river, and crosses it mid way between Llanrwst and Betws y Coed, before continuing along the hillside of Gwydyr Forest to Betws y Coed [15 miles], crossing the river Llugwy just prior to the station.

Betws y Coed was the largest station on the line and consisted of two lengthy platforms which were rarely utilised to the full. A Refreshment Room and station offices stood on the Up side platform. Access to the Down platform was by a covered footbridge, which adjoined a semi open wooden building that provided some shelter. Behind the Down platform was the goods yard., No.1. signal cabin stood at the north end of the station on the Down side and No.2. signal box, also on the Down side south of the platforms, where the single line commenced.

Half a mile beyond the station the line begins to climb in earnest, initially at a gradient of 1 in 50, changing to 1 in 69 half way up and on which is Beaver Pool tunnel, 117 yards long. The gradient continues at 1 in 56 and turns west leaving the Conwy Valley to enter the Lledr Valley. Levelling off to 1 in 220, the line passes over Gethin's Bridge ($17\frac{1}{4}$ miles), a structure of seven small arches and one large, plus a length of blank stone wall. This viaduct carries the line across the river Lledr, another tributary of the Conwy, and away from the Gwydyr Forest, along the edge of which it has passed for nearly $2\frac{3}{4}$ miles. The line takes a somewhat tortuous course in a generally westerly direction on a still rising gradient of 1 in 47, the steepest on the line and which extends for a distance of $1\frac{3}{4}$ miles and near the end of which is the 148 yards long Pont-y-pant Lower tunnel. Beyond this is Pont-y-pant station ($22\frac{1}{2}$ miles) which consists of a single platform, on the Down side, with a substantial station building. The station had a Down siding and an Up loop, but these were removed on 28th July 1957. At one time the loop, sidings and signals were controlled from a signal box on the up side, but this was removed before the Second World War. Pont-y-pant was an intermediate station in the section from Betws y Coed to Dolwyddelan and not a block or

4. Betws y Coed. c. **1956**. An Up Derby 'Lightweight' D.M.U. in early livery with 'cat's whiskers' pulls into the platform. Note the Camping Coach in the goods yard, providing a very popular holiday arrangement offered by British Railways, now discontinued. The covered footbridge, and the Down platform fencing are freshly painted giving a well cared for appearance. *H.Rogers Jones.*

token post.

On leaving Pont-y-pant station the line changes direction, this time heading south west, and the gradient evens out to 1 in 304 and then 1 in 126, on the first part of which is the 66 yard Pont-y-pant Upper tunnel. Beyond this the line falls at 1 in 330 for 500 yards, followed by a stretch of level track, which gives the fireman a brief respite, before running into Dolwyddelan station (24 miles). This is a token exchange point with a passing loop. The station consists of an island platform, access for passengers being by means of a stairs connected to the road overbridge. There was a large goods shed and siding on the Up side, and a goods loop on the Down side, the building being demolished in the late 1950s and replaced by a very small shed. Originally there was a signal cabin here, but this was removed and the frame relocated at the Blaenau end of the station building on the platform. This was also the last passing place before Blaenau Ffestiniog. At one time a quarry line ran alongside the down goods loop, transhipping of slate taking place. It is shown on the 1914 edition 25" to 1 mile Ordnance Survey map although unfortunately no photograph appears to have been taken when the quarry was working.

Beyond Dolwyddelan the scenery becomes wild and desolate as the line climbs at 1 in 62 for about a mile and a quarter, before easing slightly to 1 in 90 for a short distance, at Bertheos tunnel, 47 yards long. After this a levelling off takes place towards Roman Bridge (25³/₄ miles) which has a single platform on the Down side with station buildings similar in design to Pont-y-pant. Tickets were collected here for passengers travelling to Blaenau. A short siding was located on the Down side just before the platform, but this too was removed in 1957. Beyond the station is a short tunnel 43 yards long, the portal bearing the date 1891, which causes some confusion, as the Festiniog tunnel carries the date 1879. The explanation is that originally the tunnel was built unlined and quite literally was just a hole in the rock. Twelve years later it was found necessary to add lining and the date of completion was added to commemorate this.

Beyond this short tunnel, the gradient stiffens to 1 in 60 for

about a mile and a half to the northern portal of the Festiniog tunnel, where it abruptly turns south east. The tunnel is straight apart from a few yards at the north end, and passengers in a south bound DMU can see through to the other end, over two miles distant. About a quarter of a mile before the end of the tunnel the line reaches its summit, 790 feet above sea level and 26¹/₂ miles from Llandudno Junction. It then falls at 1 in 600 to just beyond the tunnel mouth where Greaves and Oakley Sidings were situated. Here the gradient drops at 1 in 43 and 1 in 144, followed by a short rise of 1 in 100 before coming level to the point where the original Blaenau Ffestiniog station (27¹/₄ miles), or Blaenau Ffestiniog North, as it was known in British Railways days, was located.

Accidents

On 5th July 1904 two miles south of Tal-y-Cafn, the 10.25am passenger train from Llandudno to Betws y Coed became derailed, and despite the fact that the engine and train of seven six-wheeled coaches were thrown about, only one person, the driver, Charles Jones, was seriously hurt, but subsequent recovery enabled him to drive again. The locomotive, which was an L.N.W.R. 4' 6", 2-4-2 side tank engine number **891**, was turned completely round and landed in a bog, requiring the services of eight other locomotives pulling on a wire rope to extricate it. At the Official enquiry, conducted by Colonel Yorke for the Board of Trade, the cause of the accident was held to be excessive speed. The train was keeping to time, being booked at 60 mph. It was fortunate that inclement weather had inhibited passengers from travelling, the train containing only six passengers at the time. The Colonel placed no blame on any man, but condemned the use of tank engines of this type being run at more than 40 mph. *The Weekly News* dated Friday July 8th 1904, reporting on the accident located it 'exactly opposite Bodhyfryd, which is situated on the hillside, at the foot of which is the main road from which the railway is separated by a narrow field'. It added that this was not the first accident that had occurred at this spot, for some five or six years previously, a train had been derailed under very similar circumstances and within a few yards of the same place. The train was, on that occasion, negotiating the curves from the Llanrwst end, and the blame was placed on the severe flooding that occurred from time to time in this locality.

A driver sustained injuries in an accident at Dolwyddelan goods shed in 1952 when he leaned out of the cab of a Stanier 2-6-2T, to observe the shunter's signals, and collided with the door pillar. The accident was attributed to the driver forgetting that he was on a wider locomotive than the type which usually worked the turn, clearance being less than usual.

An unusual accident occurred on Wednesday 29th October 1958 when an Ivatt 2-6-2T working the 6.30am Class K freight from Llandudno Junction to Blaenau Festiniog North was derailed by a kitten at the converging points at the south end of the station. The kitten became wedged in the points and its body prevented the point blades from making

5. Betws y Coed.12th July 1965. The daily freight train with Ivatt Class 2 2-6-2T No.**41233** of Llandudno Junction shed, returning from Blaenau Ffestiniog, draws slowly to a halt by the water column on its leisurely journey home. The Up platform canopy support brackets were identical to those at Llanberis station. The station is still very tidy and cared for. *C.L.Caddy.*

proper contact. The incident caused disruption to the services and it was four hours before the Llandudno Junction breakdown crew, using hydraulic jacks, returned the locomotive to the rails. The freight working continued from Llanrwst about 2/00pm.

Train Services

The initial train services consisted of five through trains daily between Blaenau and Llandudno Junction, the workings being manned by traincrews from Llandudno Junction and the small sub shed at Blaenau. There were also two intermediate workings between Llandudno Junction and Betws y Coed. The first trains in each direction crossed at Llanrwst, with the second workings crossing at Dolwyddelan. Mail trains first appeared on the line on 1st May **1880**, and subsequently ran daily, including Sundays.

The earliest Working Time Table to hand is dated July, August & September **1904**, when seven passenger trains worked each way between Llandudno Junction and Blaenau. There were additional trains that worked from the Junction or Blaenau to Betws y Coed. The first and last through workings daily between the Junction and Blaenau were run as mixed trains, and although there was no corresponding Up mixed working, a mixed train ran in the evenings from Blaenau to Betws y Coed, carrying workmen. First Down train departed at 4.25am, arriving at Blaenau at 6.12am. It is listed in the Public Time Table for the same period and running in the same times. There was one Sunday working in each direction, departing 5.10am from Llandudno Junction, which carried passengers and mail, and which had a twelve hour layover at Blaenau before working the evening passenger back. It is understood that there were eight sets of men based with the shed at Blaenau Festiniog at this time.

The Sunday working was still shown in the public time tables for April 1st to July 10th **1915** when seven trains ran daily in each direction, with two additional Down trains on a Saturday, but with no balancing Up passenger journeys. By July **1919** the Sunday work had been withdrawn although seven through journeys in each direction formed the passenger service, with four Down and three Up trips between the Junction and Betws y Coed. There was one through freight in each direction, and one goods in each direction from the Junction to Betws y Coed. The July 1921 Working Time Table shows an increase to 9 trains each way, which included a seasonal excursion that did not run on Saturdays, and two through freight trains each way daily. In addition there were four Down trains to Betws y Coed but only one in the Up direction. The last Down train daily ran to Betws, where it parked the stock and worked back L.E. to the Junction. The Saturday times were later than the weekday ones. By July **1923** the through journeys remained at nine Down trips and eight Up trips, with two goods trips each way; five passenger trains worked from the Junction to Betws, but only two worked back. The last train of the day which only ran on Thursdays, Fridays and Saturdays worked back Empty Stock. An additional freight worked south to Betws, where it shunted for 90 minutes before working back with an Up freight. There was little change by 1926. Blaenau Ffestiniog shed closed in September 1931, the men and work being transferred to Llandudno Junction. In April 1934 the number of weekday trains on the branch remained at nine in each direction, with four extra trains on a Saturday. There were five trains between Llandudno Junction and Betws y Coed and return during weekdays, some of which were motor trains, and an additional late train

on Saturday nights. Stock for the 7.40am Up was parked overnight at Blaenau and a light engine departed Llandudno Junction at 5.50am daily for this. The last Down train from Blaenau worked back to Betws at 9/55pm on weekdays, where it attached to the 10/25pm passenger to the Junction. On Saturdays after working the 9/40pm from Llandudno Junction to Blaenau, after parking the stock, it departed there at 11/25pm as far as Betws, before attaching to the empty motor train and departing at midnight for the Junction. Sunday trains had also reappeared for the low summer season as far as Betws y Coed, with four trains shown working from Chester, the Junction or Llandudno, and a path for a fifth evening train, which by all accounts ran regularly. Two of the trips were worked by motor train.

The freight Working Time Table for September **1933** shows two trains daily from the Junction, with 'suspended' paths provided for another three trains daily, one of which nevertheless ran regularly.

As the country emerged from the 1930's depression by the summer of **1939**, traffic on the line was at its peak, and showed eleven trains each way on weekdays, with an additional late train on Thursdays, some of which worked from and to Llandudno. In addition there were seven trains to and from Betws, again some working from Llandudno. On Saturdays, this increased to sixteen for Blaenau, but only fourteen from there to Betws, Llandudno or the Junction, and the balance was worked back as Empty Stock workings. On Sundays there were five trains to Blaenau, of which two worked from Llandudno, and another four as far as Betws, balanced by four Up trains to Llandudno from Blaenau as well as two Empty Stock trains to the Junction, and three from Betws to Llandudno. The freight traffic for the same period showed paths for four through freight trains to Blaenau and return, two of which were suspended paths, together with a daily working to Betws y Coed and return, a suspended SO path to Llanrwst and return and two 'Q' SX paths to Tal-y-Cafn, but only one return 'Q' SX path. The first freight train of the day also had a 'Q' path from Blaenau to Greaves and Oakeley Quarries sidings and back before returning with the Up freight.

The wartime Emergency Working Time Table, issued on 11th September **1939** curtailed services drastically, although the line fared better than most other branches. This showed seven through workings in each direction, with no short trips. There were no extra Saturday workings and the Sunday trains had also been removed. The last Down train left the Junction at 6/40pm and returned on the 8/10pm from Blaenau. By October **1940**, there was a more even distribution of trains, the last Down train departing Llandudno Junction at 8/50pm and returning as Empty Stock during the week, but a Class 'B' passenger on Saturdays, running in the same times, departed Blaenau at 10/20pm. There was an extra working to Betws and return on weekdays, which was extended to Blaenau and return on a Saturday. By **1943** this had been reduced by one train daily each way, although the last train from Blaenau now worked back as passenger on weekdays as well as Saturdays. The freight service was also cut back to one train per day to Blaenau and return in the morning, and a mid day freight to Llanrwst and return. There was a suspended unbalanced freight path from Blaenau to Llandudno Junction with no indication on how it would be worked so presumably the 7.57am Down passenger working would have been double headed. By June **1947** there was a daily through freight which departed Llandudno Junction at 6.45am and which arrived at Blaenau at 10.30am. It returned at 12/45pm, arriving at the Junction at 4/20pm. On

Mondays, Wednesdays and Fridays, a second freight departed for Blaenau at 8.55am, reaching its destination at 1/55pm, returning from there at 2/40pm and home by 6/30pm. On Tuesdays and Thursdays Only, it departed Llandudno Junction at the same time, and ran in the same path as far as Betws y Coed, where it terminated, working back from there at 12/45pm reaching the Junction at 2/43pm. There was also a daily 'Q' path from Blaenau to Greaves Siding at 11.10am where it shunted for ten minutes before working back to Blaenau. There was no mention of Oakeley Siding.

By the summer of **1948** the passenger service had increased to ten Down trains through to Blaenau, from Llandudno or the Junction, but only nine Up trains during the week, with a daily Empty Stock and SX passenger working to Betws, balanced by two return passenger workings to Llandudno Junction. Freight services were the same as 1947. The winter service for **1951** showed nine trains daily each way with an additional SX working from Llandudno Junction to Betws y Coed and return. The freight pattern was similar to 1947 except that departure times from Blaenau varied alternate days. The daily goods departed at 12/45pm on Tuesdays, Thursdays and Saturdays, but when the second Down freight worked through to Blaenau on Mondays, Wednesdays and Fridays, departure of the first goods was delayed until after the second freight arrived, departing at 1/04pm.

The summer season commencing 14th June **1954** gave nine weekday departures daily to Blaenau and return, with two additional trips to Betws y Coed and return in the afternoon, at 2/16pm and 4/48pm. On Thursdays there was an extra late departure from Llandudno at 10/50pm to Betws, which returned as Empty Stock. On Saturdays there were two extra workings to Blaenau and return, the first of these running in the same path as the 4/48pm which returned as the 6/36pm from Blaenau. The late train on Saturdays departed Llandudno at 10/50pm and worked back as Empty Stock from Blaenau at 12.37am on Sunday mornings. On the freight workings for the same period this had been reduced to one train each way daily.

The introduction of Diesel Multiple Units to the line in March **1956** showed no significant alteration to the service either in frequency or in running times, although an additional train ran from the Junction to Betws and return in the evening. By the summer of 1958, there was an additional working in the morning from Llandudno Junction to Betws y Coed and return, as well as the three short workings as previously mentioned. However an innovation was the introduction of four Sunday workings from Llandudno to Betws y Coed and return, which ran for eight Sundays. There was no change to the freight workings. In **1960** there was a modest increase, with ten trains running to Blaenau daily, with an additional three to Betws y Coed and return. There was the usual late train at 11/00pm to Blaenau on Thursday nights, returning as E.C.S., whilst on Saturdays the 5/03pm to Betws was extended as previously to Blaenau returning from there at 6/30pm and the 11/00pm ran as on Thursdays. On Sundays there were now five trains to Betws y Coed and return from Llandudno. The Winter 1960 Working Time Table showed ten trains daily to Blaenau and return and one evening train to Betws y Coed and return during the week. On Saturdays there was an additional DMU to Betws at 4/42pm, returning from there at 5/40pm. There was no late train on Saturdays as previously.

By the summer of **1961** there had been an increase in the number of trains run during the week, with 12 trips Mondays to

Fridays to Blaenau and return, and two trips to Betws y Coed and return. On Saturdays there were thirteen to Blaenau and return, but only one to Betws y Coed. The extra working was the 10/50pm from Llandudno, which returned early Sunday morning as an Empty DMU. There were once again five trips from Llandudno to Betws y Coed and return on Sundays, but only for five weeks. By the commencement of winter services on 11th September 1961, the service had been reduced to ten trips to Blaenau with one additional working to Betws y Coed during the week, and an additional trip to Betws and return at 4/42pm on Saturdays. However the freight traffic was increased to three trains daily between Llandudno Junction and Blaenau, with one trip working in a 'Q' path, as required. The first working departed from the Junction at 6.30am and worked non stop to Betws y Coed, where it waited for thirty minutes before continuing non stop to Blaenau, where it was due at 8.30am. It remained there as required, returning to Llandudno Junction at 12/40pm S) and 1/20pm SX. The second freight departed the Junction at 8.25am and stopped at all stations to Blaenau, arriving there at 11.00am. It was diagrammed to work to Betws y Coed as Engine and Brake Van only, returning to Blaenau at 2/20pm, calling at Dolwyddelan for ten minutes in a 'Q' path, [as required]. It returned to the Junction at 5/04pm SX, 1/20pm SO.

The summer **1962** passenger service was similar to the previous year, with the Sunday trains running on five days. The freight working was the same as the previous winter. Winter 1962 saw the passenger service reduced to nine trains to Blaenau and return, and one afternoon working to Betws y Coed and back. The freight service was altered with two trains running to Blaenau with a 'Q' path for train mid morning, which was suspended. The first train departed Llandudno Junction at 6.30am Mondays to Saturdays. On Mondays to Fridays it worked back to Betws y Coed at 12/40pm, where it crossed with the second SX freight train that departed Llandudno Junction at 11.30am. The first remained at Betws for 65 minutes before continuing to Llandudno Junction, arriving there at 4/57pm. On Saturdays it departed Blaenau at 1/20pm and worked straight through to the Junction. Meanwhile the 11.30am from the Junction stood at Betws for 70 minutes before moving on to Blaenau, where it worked as required from 3/10pm until 5/04pm whence it returned to the Junction, arriving there at 7/09pm.

The summer services which commenced on 17th June **1963** saw a drastic reduction of trains on the line, only six DMUs working daily between Llandudno Junction and Blaenau with an early morning short trip from Blaenau to Dolwyddelan and return. There was no variation on Saturdays. Sunday services were reduced to four trains between Llandudno and Betws y Coed and return, but the season was extended over nine weeks. The freight time table remained the same as the previous winter. There was no change with the introduction of winter services on 9th September 1963 to passenger or freight workings.

The new link line connecting the former L.N.W.R. branch from Blaenau Ffestiniog North with the G.W.R. line at Blaenau Ffestiniog Central over part of the Festiniog Railway trackbed was officially opened on 20th April 1964, and extended to a point close to the Nuclear Power Station, where a siding with an overhead gantry crane was provided to lift the nuclear fuel flasks from road hauled vehicles onto the special bogie rail wagons. The line was terminated short of the original Trawsfynydd station. The cost of the link line connecting the two stations at Blaenau was met by Liverpool Corporation who had obtained permission to flood the Treweryn valley, thereby causing the G.W.R. Bala to Festiniog line to close. It is interesting that a proposal to divert the G.W.R. branch was made in 1957 but it was estimated that the cost would have exceeded £1 million. The cheaper alternative was to link the two lines at the northern end and sever the line to Bala. This was covered by the Liverpool Waterworks Act of 1957, and the B.T.C. Act of 1959 authorised the construction of the link line. The G.W.R. branch closed to passenger traffic on 4th January 1960, and freight traffic from Bala ceased on 28th January 1961. The intermediate stations from Blaenau Ffestiniog Central to Trawsfynydd were closed permanently from 4th May 1964, although arrangements had been in force to keep the intermediate stations open for freight handling until then, using road vehicles. The link line and reconnected ex G.W.R. tracks to Trawsfynydd was officially opened on 20th April 1964. It is not known whether any traffic to the intermediate stations was ever handled in the brief period between the Official re-opening of the line and the closure of the stations to general freight traffic a month later.

The summer services for **1964**, introduced on 15th June showed a slight improvement on the passenger workings, with seven trains each way daily, and four workings for the nine Sundays from July 5th between Llandudno and Betws y Coed. The freight service was reduced to one train daily from the Junction to Blaenau and return. The 7th September 1964 saw the introduction of winter services, with a reversion to six trains daily. The solitary freight appeared for the last time in freight working time tables. On 7th December 1964 the remaining L.M.S. branch lines in North Wales closed either wholly, or in part, with some residual work surviving on truncated sections. This was followed a few weeks later by the closure to passenger services between Ruabon and Morfa Mawddach, with the line to Llangollen remaining open for limited freight traffic for a brief period before it too was strangled out of existence.

June **1965** saw a mid day train reinstated together with three Sunday trains from Llandudno to Betws y Coed for nine weeks. Freight traffic was removed from the Working Time Tables and was shown as a trip working, to be found in the Chester District Shunting and Trip Working Notices. This was shown as one train daily, extended to Trawsfynydd as required, to pick up the nuclear fuel flasks, which were, and are, worked to and from Sellafield, and are the main reason for the line remaining open to this day.

The old practice of issuing two passenger working time tables each year had been dispensed with, and one issue for passenger traffic sufficed, although two issues for freight persisted. The 1966 books were issued on 18th April and lasted until 5th March 1967. The train service remained as previously, with the 13.19pm from Llandudno Junction to Blaenau and the 14.25pm return working running from 27th June to 3rd September only. From 1st September however, the 20.17pm Llandudno Junction to Blaenau and corresponding 21.55pm Blaenau to Llandudno Junction ran on Saturdays only and the Sunday services did not appear. This was repeated with only minor

timing changes in the issue, which ran from 6th March 1967 to 5th May 1968, and again in the issue dated 6th May 1968 to 4th May 1969. Again, the middle day train ran from late June to early September. In 1969 the usual middle day seasonal working had advanced to 13.35pm from Llandudno Junction and 14.35pm from Blaenau. The rest of the passenger working was as for previous years.

From 4th May **1970**, the practice of keeping passenger and freight trains to separate publications was dispensed with and were replaced by Mandatory and Conditional Time Tables. The Mandatory issues covered the twelve months from early May, whilst the Conditional Time Tables [which covered mainly freight workings] were issued twice a year, approximately six months apart. Five trains daily sufficed for the greater part of the year, with an extra late evening working on Saturdays. During summer months, this was expanded to seven trains. This was repeated in 1971 and 1972. In 1971, Glan Conwy reappeared in the Time Tables. In 1973, there was no change to the weekday pattern of services in winter or summer, but three Sunday trains ran from Llandudno, two to Blaenau Ffestiniog and the middle one to Betws y Coed from 1st July to 2nd September inclusive. However these are shown in the Working Time Tables as 'Not Advertised'!

The **1974** time table saw a reduction during the winter period from five trains daily during the week, to four, with the Saturdays Only evening train running in the same times. There was a very large gap between the 08.17am departure and 15.45pm from 6th October onwards. As before, the summer Sunday trains remained unadvertised. **1975** followed the same pattern with only four trains weekdays in the winter. The Summer Sunday only workings, running from 29th June to 31st August were increased to four trains from Llandudno at 11.00am, 14.05pm and 15.55pm to Blaenau, and the 18.30pm to Betws y Coed. The note 'Not Advertised' was removed from this issue. **1976** issues saw a relapse, with only four weekday trains in the winter months. The

6. Llandudno Junction. July 1955. Jubilee No.**45620** *North Borneo* working the second part of the 8.05am from Euston to Holyhead, running on the Down slow line from Colwyn Bay and over an hour late, passes the 12/27pm from Blaenau Ffestiniog with **41236,** which is held at the Outer Home signal. The Holyhead train was not booked to stop at the Junction and took the Goods avoiding line through the station, and once out of section, the branch train proceeded to the bay platform.
H. Rogers Jones.

Saturday Only evening train no longer ran. The Sunday trains did not appear either.

The layout and print style of the Conditional issues of the Working Time Tables dated 4th October 1976 and the Mandatory issue Time Tables dated 2nd May 1977 to 7th May 1978 were revised. The number of trains was increased to five daily during the winter months, and seven from 27th June to 3rd September. There were no Sunday trains. The following year the winter period remained the same, but the summer period, from 19th June to 9th September indicated eight trains on weekdays but only seven on Saturdays. **1979** saw nine trains daily, Mondays to Fridays in each direction with seven trains on a Saturday in the summer period from 18th June to 7th September. The winter period remained as before, with five trains each way. The issue dated 12th May **1980** to 10th May 1981 was the last one produced under the Mandatory and Conditional series. The summer period from 16th June to 5th September saw nine trains each way from Mondays to Fridays and seven on Saturdays, reverting to five for the winter period.

From 1st June 1981, Passenger and Freight Working Time Tables were re-introduced. The service was unchanged from the previous year. The same was true for 1982 and 1983 but in case of the latter the summer season 11.05am SX from Llandudno and the 13.30pm from Blaenau Ffestiniog to Llandudno were loco hauled stock and not DMU. From 14th May 1984, the train frequency remained the same, with nine trains on weekdays, with the 11.05am and 14.53pm SX from Llandudno, returning with the 13.30pm and 16.25pm SX from Blaenau worked by loco hauling vacuum braked stock. On Saturdays in the summer period, the seven trips were worked with DMUs. The winter period reverted to five trains daily.

The **1985** issue, dated 13th May to 11th May 1986, showed the summer weekday period with two of the nine weekday workings running as loco hauled vacuum braked trains and in approximately the same timings as in past years. On summer Saturdays, there were eight DMU workings each way. Sunday services were reintroduced from 21st July to 25th August with three trains between Llandudno and Blaenau. The winter service remained unchanged.

A revised Passenger Working Time Table was issued dated 30th September 1985 to 11th May 1986. The Llandudno Junction to Blaenau Ffestiniog service was no longer shown separately, but was included within the main Crewe to Holyhead pages. Sprinter units were appearing on the North Wales coast but none were scheduled to work to Blaenau Ffestiniog. The normal five trains per day persisted for this period.

The Passenger Working Time Table dated 12th May **1986** to 10th May 1987 introduced Sprinter DMUs to the line, but there were technical problems and their appearance was spasmodic. Another innovative feature was that some of the workings emanated from points further afield than Llandudno Junction. The summer season 10.52am to Blaenau Ffestiniog departed from Manchester Victoria at 08.42am.

There were eight trains between Llandudno Junction and Blaenau Ffestiniog in the summer period, with the 14.40pm Llandudno to Ffestiniog and the 16.05pm to Llandudno worked SX by loco hauled stock in lieu of the Sprinter. The winter workings were reduced to five trains daily. Gwynedd County Council paid for the three Sunday trains that worked from and to Llandudno for the six peak weeks in July and August. The following year saw the same eight train workings, mostly using Sprinter units. The 10.51am from Llandudno Junction 2D15 started from Crewe at 09.19am. whilst the 17.47pm from Blaenau Ffestiniog attached to the front of the 18.10pm from Holyhead and worked to Crewe. The winter service reverted to five trains daily. Three Sunday trains from Llandudno to Blaenau Ffestiniog and return, sponsored by Gwynedd County Council, ran from 26th July to 30th August.

The issue dated 16th May **1988** to 14th May 1989 had a few changes in the timings, but the trains were worked by the older D.M.Units, and not Sprinters. There was the same frequency of five winter and eight summer journeys in each direction. The summer 12.23pm working from the Junction originated at Birmingham New Street at 09.28am. and worked via Crewe and Chester. The same Sunday service operated from 17th July to 4th September - two weeks longer than the previous year.

In the **1989** Issue, dated 15th May 1989 to 13th May 1990, The Wednesday & Friday only freight from Llandudno Junction to Trawsfynydd, 6D38 is shown for the first time, departing the Junction at 07.05am and arriving at Trawsfynydd at 08.56am. It departed on the return journey from Trawsfynydd at 12.48pm and arrived at the Junction at 14.21pm. The Sprinters were not rostered to work on the line. There was a change to the winter schedules from 5th October. The 20.42 from Llandudno Junction to Blaenau and the corresponding 21.49pm return working, which was daily during the summer period continued to run on Thursdays, Fridays and Saturdays. There was a variation of the Gwynedd County Council sponsored Sunday trains, which ran from 9th July until 10th September. Two trains ran to Blaenau and

7. Pont y pant. 1953. Stanier 2-6-2T **40130** working the 10.54am Blaenau Ffestiniog to Llandudno threads through the Lledr valley heading for home. The fireman has been active as the black smoke suggests, which hangs over the valley dispersing amongst the trees. The Stanier Class 3 tanks worked the line almost exclusively from about 1946 until replaced by the Ivatt Class 2, tank engine, which were themselves replaced by DMUs in 1956.   *H. Rogers Jones.*

back, but the 14.45pm from Llandudno only worked to Betws y Coed, arriving there at 15.22pm. It returned at 15.28pm to Llandudno.

The Working Time Tables issued on 14th May **1990** now contained the Freight Workings and from this date Saturday Services along the coast were shown separately. Trawsfynydd was now included in the main time tables. The experimental working with the Sunday trains by Gwynedd County Council, extended from Blaenau to Trawsfynydd in 1989 had proved successful and two workings formed the Sunday services. However the early afternoon trip to Betws y Coed was dropped. The section from Blaenau Ffestiniog to Trawsfynydd was not advertised by British Rail. Seven trains ran daily during the summer months. The 20.49 from Llandudno to Blaenau ran until 28th September and came off for the winter. The Freight to Trawsfynydd ran five minutes later than during the previous year, on Wednesdays and Fridays with the same running time, and the return journey commenced slightly earlier. A Sundays Reissued supplement came into force on 7th October 1990, but did not affect the branch.

Pre war small consignments traffic was carried over the branch in Tariff vans. A 96 page publication entitled *List of Tariff Vans* ERO 29566 stamped July 1935 gave operating instructions, listed the stations served and specified by which trains the Tariff vans were scheduled. Van 42 ran from Curzon Street, Birmingham to Blaenau Ffestiniog as required., Van 144 from Chester to Blaenau Ffestiniog, van 297 from Liverpool (Park Lane) to Blaenau Ffestiniog and van 346 from Manchester (Liverpool Road) to Blaenau. Vans 62 and 63 ran from Blaenau Ffestiniog to Chester. When van 42 worked, it was attached to the 10.55am from Llandudno Junction. Vans 297 and 346 ran daily, attached to the 6.50am from Llandudno Junction. In the reverse direction, vans 62 and 63 ran daily, the former attached to the 10.25am to the Junction, whilst van 63 was attached to the 2/10pm Up working. Both worked forward to Chester attached to the 7/20pm Menai Bridge to Mold Junction. From Manchester, van 346a also worked daily to Blaenau Ffestiniog but travelled via the 5.45am Ruabon to Blaenau via Bala and over the Great Western route.

The L. M. S. issued a publication entitled *Instructions for dealing with Parcels Traffic*, ERO 21229, dated November 1938 which covered the Western Division traffic specified the exact routing of Newspaper and Parcels traffic flow. There were no through workings of Parcels or News vans along the Conwy Valley and whatever traffic was consigned up the valley was transhipped at Llandudno Junction to the timetabled passenger trains under the control of the guard. Some examples from the Down line traffic which had consignments to places up the valley included the 1.10am SO Kensington to Crewe (Messrs Lyons' Traffic - summer only) lists van 6 as CBR which worked forward to Bangor on the 5.02am passenger to Holyhead, calling at most stations. Consignments for the Conwy valley line were transferred at Llandudno Junction and worked forward by the 8.07am to destination in the care of the Passenger guard. The 2.35am Express from Euston to Liverpool had van 8a, which was CBR worked forward from Crewe to Bangor on the 7.40am to Holyhead. This carried parcels traffic for the branch which was transferred at Llandudno Junction onto the 10.11am. The 1.30am SuO Parcels from Stafford to Crewe included CBR vans off the 7/50pm from Euston to Llandudno [van 6] and to Bangor [van 7] and the 11/30pm Birmingham to Bangor [van 9] with branch traffic transferred from van 9 at the Junction. The 8/55pm SX parcels Euston to Manchester had van numbers 6 for Llandudno,

which included transfers for the branch, and van 7 was for Bangor. The 10/40pm SX Euston to Manchester, carrying News and Parcels, had CBR van 7 transferred at Crewe to the 2.45am to Bangor, and had Conwy Valley consignments transferred at the Junction. Newspaper traffic was chiefly carried on the 1.25am Manchester Exchange to Chester which worked forward attached to the 2.05am from Crewe to Holyhead. Through consignments were in van 2, but most of the news was for wholesalers, who sorted and labelled their consignments on Chester platform, and van 3 was primarily for this traffic. The front part of the 2.05am from Crewe conveyed parcel and letter post for Ireland, with van 2 being the TPO sorting van from Birmingham. Van 4 carried News. Van 5 carried mail, van 6 carried fish, van 7 carried parcels traffic and van 8 carried news. The three vans from Manchester were attached to the rear of the 2.05am from Crewe, becoming vans 7, 8 and 9. Provision was made for principal passenger trains throughout the system to be able to carry mail, news and parcel traffic during the day, and reduce congestion at main line centres.

The only Up traffic train which catered for the various branch lines and points that fed into the main Holyhead to Crewe line was the 7/40pm Holyhead to Birmingham, with the London traffic transferred at Crewe for Euston. Of course the 'Irish Mails' had through workings from Holyhead, and picked up and set down mail at specified lineside apparatus along the route. Vans that had worked Down the branches, were returned back to the main line at Bangor, Llandudno Junction, Rhyl or Chester, where they were attached to the two 'Horse and Carriage' stock trains that worked daily in the Up direction to Crewe or Ordsall Lane.

Coach Workings

The Conwy Valley line in steam days rarely used corridor stock in the make up of the regular trains, as workings were purely local. The circuit sets were all based on Llandudno Junction and details were specified in the *'Diagram of Carriage Working'*, which the L.N.W.R. and L.M.S. produced in printed book form until 1933, after which, Roneo sheets were used. The earliest Diagram of Carriage Working available is dated September 21st 1925. The Conwy Valley line workings came under the title Llandudno Junction and Blaenau Festiniog sets, worked as Circuit sets 819 - 822, in rotation. Each set comprised 5 vehicles, 63 tons total weight which covered the time tabled requirements, Some workings were strengthened and sets of vehicles for such purposes were allocated set numbers. Circuits 830, 841 and 842. were used on the line. Demands over and above this were provided from a pool of stock at the district carriage centres, or could be requested from the Chief General Superintendent at Crewe. Whenever a coach within a set was due for overhaul its place was taken by a replacement vehicle, but the circuit set make up remained approximately the same. In the 1925 circuit diagrams six wheel vehicles were used in the Llandudno Junction and Blaenau Festiniog sets. In time these were replaced with non corridor bogie stock and the numbers of vehicles in a circuit set were reduced, but the seating capacity remained approximately the same.

By 1933, the six wheel stock had been withdrawn from regular traffic use although a set was retained for Workmen's trains. Now the Llandudno Junction and Blaenau Festiniog circuit comprised 5 sets, numbered 833-837, each set comprised two vehicles - 50 tons. Circuit set number 852 comprised two third brake and two third class six wheel vehicles, 52 tons, which worked the quarrymens train to and from Blaenau Ffestiniog. An Inter District set, No.174 comprising 3 vehicles, 84 tons, based on Chester, worked the 3/47pm to Blaenau and back before returning to Chester Mondays to Fridays. Another Inter District Set, No.172C worked two trips between Llandudno Junction and Betws y Coed as part of its circuit, which was a three day working, starting at Llandudno and finishing at Caernarvon on day one. On day two it worked from Caernarvon to Llanberis, then to Llandudno Junction. The third day it started at the Junction and worked between Llandudno and Llanberis, finishing its work at Llandudno. It then started the same three day circuit again. Another vehicle on the Conwy Valley line was the Observation coach which plied between Llandudno and Blaenau Ffestiniog. It's circuit number was 1330 and it started and finished at Llandudno working daily the morning trip to Blaenau and return, and an afternoon trip to Betws y Coed and back to Llandudno.

After 1933 information about circuit sets are hard to come by. By 1938 the remaining Workmens' six wheel set had been withdrawn. All workings before 1939 were undertaken with L.N.W.R. non corridor stock which was itself replaced by Stanier non corridor stock over the years. In the summer season, the Observation coach worked on the line and this persisted until the D.M.U.s replaced the steam workings in 1956.

Rolling Stock Diagrams were prepared for each of the Divisions on the L.M.S. or London Midland Region and specified the normal circuit sets of rolling stock required for the time tabled trains. These were revised twice a year.

Rolling stock for extra and additional traffic workings over and above the regular scheduled services in the timetables, for seasonal and Guaranteed Excursions etc. were supplied by the Divisional Operating Superintendent and details were given in **'Supplementary and Weekly Rolling Stock Diagram Notices'** sometimes referred to as R.S.D. notices.

Supplementary Notices to the original Diagram were issued as required and outlining changes, and remained valid until the commencement of the next Diagram revision. The Western Division Supplementary Notices were identified by the code E.R.O. 53022/4. **Carriage Workings for Special and Additional Trains** [code ERO 53022/3 for Western Division and ERO 53022/4 for the Midland Division], were issued from May to end of September with additional issues for the Easter and Christmas periods,. The layout and form of the books changed little over the years and lasted well into B.R. days. Each additional working was allocated a Clause number, the Train working being identified from the points worked to and from, with the arrival and departure times. A description of the train was given, which specified a Reporting Number, where one was allocated, and previous and successive clause numbers were added. Clause numbers started afresh each week and Clause 5 in one week was not the same as Clause 5 the previous or following week. Typical examples are as follows:

In the R.S.D. Notice No.9 dated Friday July 22nd to Thursday July 28th 1938, a Guaranteed Excursion ran from Blaenau Ffestiniog to Glasgow and return, Clause 187, made up of 1-CBB, 2-QF, KC, 4-QF, KC, 2-QF and CH. The stock worked to Llandudno Junction the previous day, and unfortunately no details are available. The empty stock worked from Llandudno Junction at 9/30pm to Blaenau Festiniog, arriving there at 10.28pm and the Excursion departed at 11/00pm. Arrival time at, and departure from Glasgow was not specified, but the Excursion

arrived at Blaenau Ffestiniog at 8.21am on Sunday, 24th July. It departed ten minutes later as Empty Stock for Llandudno Junction, arriving there at 9.27am and working forward at an unspecified time to Holyhead. The stock remained at Holyhead until Tuesday 26th July when it worked as Clause 822 to Folkestone, departing at 1.20am. From Folkestone it worked as E.C.S. to Willesden. Times of the movement on Southern metals were not given. Two Class 3P 2-6-2T worked the stock on the branch in both directions. At Llandudno Junction they were replaced by an unspecified 5XP.

On Saturday 23rd July 1938, a Sunday School Excursion comprising Circuit Stock 2122 (8.B. made up to 10.B.) running as Clause 432 departed Llandudno Junction at 6.20am and arrived at Blaenau Ffestiniog at 7.23am. It left for Llandudno with 240 adults and 260 children at 8.15am, arriving at 9.31am. Motive power is not known, although it is believed that an LNWR 0-6-0 'Cauliflower' was the motive power. The stock then worked its normal circuit to Chester, where it next worked the 3/10pm to Shotton and Rhyl, before working E.C.S. to Crewe as a path became available.

The return Excursion stock was specified as Clause 317 and designated Lavatory extra train, made up of 7B made up to 9B departed Crewe at 11.05am arriving at Llandudno 1/21pm. The stock was parked in the carriage sidings at Llandudno when it worked the return excursion to Blaenau Ffestiniog, arriving there at 8/42pm, and returned as Empty Stock to Llandudno carriage sidings. The following day it formed the ordinary 7/15pm working to Manchester Exchange, arriving at 9/51pm. It then worked E.C.S. to Ordsall Lane.

On Friday, 10th August 1951, Clauses 187, 188 and 190 specified three sets of Non-corridor stock (5) working Relief trains on the branch. Clause 187 worked the 7.59am Ordinary train to Blaenau Ffestiniog returning with a 9.45am Relief to Llanrwst, then 12/20pm relief to Llandudno Junction. It then worked a 4/55pm Relief to Blaenau Ffestiniog, returning to Llandudno with an Ordinary working, and then a Relief train at 11/10pm from Llandudno to Blaenau Ffestiniog and return. Clause 188 worked the 10.15am Relief and the 10/10pm Relief from Llandudno Junction to Blaenau Ffestiniog and return, whilst Clause 190 worked Relief trains between Llandudno Junction and Betws y Coed at 1/10pm and 9/30pm and return.

On Saturday, 11th August 1951 the stock that worked Clause 190 worked Clause 750, which involved the 2/16pm Relief from Llandudno Junction to Betws y Coed and return, and the 10/10pm Relief to Blaenau Ffestiniog, returning as E.C.S.. The stock which worked Clause 188 worked Clause 754 which was the 10.15am Relief and 11/10pm Relief from Llandudno Junction to Blaenau Ffestiniog and returned as E.C.S. The stock which had worked Clause 187 worked the Ordinary 7.59am to Blaenau Ffestiniog and returned with the 9.45am Relief to Llanrwst. It worked another Relief to Llandudno Junction at 12/20pm and worked back almost immediately to Betws y Coed with another Relief at 1/10pm, returning with the 2/10pm Relief to the Junction. Finally it worked yet another Relief at 9/30pm to Betws y Coed, returning to Llandudno as a Relief, before working as E.C.S. to the Junction at 11/30pm. On Sunday 12th August this same stock worked Special W640, 4/20pm from Llandudno Junction to Blaenau Ffestiniog, 6/15pm Blaenau to Llanrwst, where the train remained until 10/25pm when it worked back to Blaenau and the 11/30pm E.C.S. to Llandudno Junction.

In the late 1940s and the early 1950s the supporters of

Blaenau Ffestiniog football team, who played in a North Wales Coast league, regularly booked Guaranteed Excursion trains to travel to away fixtures. The Special Trains Notices for the period showed such workings. The usual formation was a non corridor three coach set, worked along the branch by one of the Stanier 2-6-2T that worked all the passenger workings at that time. It is believed that the locomotives and coach set worked through to their destination and return, although Bangor traincrew relieved the Llandudno Junction men when working to venues west of Caernarfon.

Restrictions & Loads of Trains

The L.M.S. and British Railways L.M.Region in common with all Railways issued publications which specified the route restrictions over which engines may or may not run, and load limits for the various classes of locomotives permitted to work over every section of line, for both passenger and freight work. Steam classes up to and including power classes 5 were authorised for Passenger trains up the Conwy Valley between Blaenau Ffestiniog and Roman Bridge, and up to Class 6 locomotives between Roman Bridge and Llandudno Junction. There were additional restrictions within the permitted classes over certain bridges and in some sidings. It was rare to find engines larger than Class 3 working the branch although when the Royal Train was parked overnight in 1953, an L.N.W.R. G2A 0-8-0 was used to haul the train to the appointed secluded spot for the overnight stop, and the train was worked forward by two Bangor 2-6-4T locomotives.

For passenger trains the line was divided in two sections. North and south of Betws y Coed the load limits applied in both Down and Up directions. Class 3 locomotives were restricted to 340 tons from Llandudno Junction to Betws y Coed. Between there and Blaenau Ffestiniog, Down trains were restricted to 155 tons, but Up trains could be loaded to 250 tons.

Freight traffic on the Conwy valley line was mostly Class 'J' or 'K'. The Booklet *'Loads of Freight Trains'* specified the loads for the respective classes of engines in each direction. The line was divided into three sections for working purposes. From Blaenau Ffestiniog to Pont-y-pant, and Pont-y-pant to Betws y Coed, the loading of class 3 locomotives, excluding brake vans was 14 wagons for Up trains and 12 for Down trains. Between Betws y Coed and Llandudno Junction this was increased to 37 wagons for Up trains and 40 for Down trains.

Signalling

The line was single throughout, worked by Electric Token Block system, with provision for crossing trains at Token Exchange points. The Sections were from Llandudno Junction No.1. to Tal-y-Cafn, 4 miles 1464 yards, the Train Staff was coloured Blue, configuration 'B'. There was no signal box here but an LMS Standard tappet frame with 15 levers was mounted on the Up platform between the shelter and the level crossing with the Electric Token instruments located in the station office on the Down platform. From Tal-y-Cafn to Llanrwst & Trefriw, 6 miles 25 yards, Train Staff coloured Red, configuration 'A'. From Llanrwst & Trefriw to Betws y Coed No.1. box, 3 miles 1581 yards, Train Staff coloured Blue, configuration 'B'. From Betws y Coed No.2. box to Dolwyddelan 5 miles 1368 yards, Train Staff coloured Red, configuration 'A' and from Dolwyddelan to Blaenau Ffestiniog, 6 miles 630 yards, Train Staff coloured Blue, configuration 'B'. Betws y Coed No.2. box was shown as a 'Staff Hut' in the Sectional Appendix to the Working Time Tables, but on the Rating Plan, was shown as a proper signal box. The signal box diagram however, designated it Betws y Coed Sidings.

Ancillary Rail Services

The outlying villages up the valley were served by the L.M.S. Country Lorry Services, which provided regular collection and delivery services to the nearest rail head. The service was developed in the thirties to combat competition from small haulers who set themselves up in direct competition to the railways. A set scale of charges was specified, based on consignment weight and the chargeable mileage. Full details were provided to potential customers in a booklet entitled '**L.M.S. Country Lorry Services**' ERO 53499/10, and the issue to hand is dated February 1939. The categories listed were Scale 'A', for small consignments and parcels up to and including 1 ton. Scale 'B' was for 2 and 4 ton loads. Scale 'C' were charges for the delivery of Grain, Flour, Oilcake and Feeding Meals and Packed Manures whilst Scale 'D' covered charges for the delivery of Basic Slag, Ground, Packed, and Packed Manure, minimum 4 tons per delivery. The Country Lorry Services came under the control of the Chief Commercial Manager, via his District Officers. North Wales as a whole came under Chester District Office. Mileages were charged from the nearest rail point, although the lorry and driver might be based several miles away.

8. Betws y Coed. July 1938. Stanier 2-6-2T No.**106** of Llandudno Junction shed (7A), draws out of the Up side yard after taking water at the tank by the former single road Locomotive shed. These tank engines were newcomers to the line at this time, and despite their indifferent steaming performance, were an improvement in crew comfort on their predecessors.   *G.H.Platt.*

Lorries based in the valley were located at Llandudno Junction, Llanrwst, Betws y Coed and Blaenau Ffestiniog. Llanrwst had two lorries attached to the Goods Yard and covered territory mainly north and east of the station. Betws y Coed also had two lorries based at the Goods Yard, and at one time the former loco shed was used as a maintenance centre for all the lorries in the valley. Betws y Coed lorries radiated mainly south of the station and into the Lledr valley as far as Roman Bridge. One lorry was based at Blaenau Ffestiniog, although it is believed that this was increased to two during the war time. The Great Western Railway also provided a Country Lorry Service, and competition was quite keen in the town. The railways in common with other road haulers who traded by carrying other persons goods were restricted by distance limits imposed by the Traffic Authority, which specified a limit of a radius of twenty five miles from their base. Most lorries were operated under a 'C' licence, although the railway did have 'B' and 'A' licenses available.

With the formation of British Railways in 1948, some of the Country Lorry Services passed to British Road Services, who also acquired most of the haulers throughout the country. Within twelve months, the smaller country depot businesses were amalgamated into larger units and so small depots closed. Blaenau Ffestiniog became the main district centre and took over some of the former G.W.R. Country Lorry Services. British Railways still retained a substantial fleet for their own use until the freight services were discontinued in the 1960s.

Special Workings

On 27th January 1956, the Divisional Operating Superintendent Mr. L.M.Sayers issued Special Notice No.93.G, which outlined Special Diesel Unit Trains - Schedule D1, commencing on February 1st and running Mondays to Fridays until further notice. This was to introduce D.M.U. working to the District and familiarise train crew with this new form of motive power. A pair of two coach lightweight units were involved. Llandudno Junction Diesel Driver and Bangor Guard worked the 8.40am to Bangor, where the Units divided. The Junction men then worked forward to Gaerwen at 9.41am and then on to Amlwch, returning from

there at 11.15am to Bangor which they reached at 12/12pm. The same driver departed Bangor at 1/10pm to Caernarvon and Afonwen, reaching there at 2/23pm and departing for Bangor at 2/35pm, arriving there at 3/55pm. After a five minute wait, it proceeded to Llandudno Junction, arriving there at 4/27pm.

Meanwhile the second unit, detached at Bangor was taken over by a Bangor Diesel driver and guard and departed back to Llandudno Junction at 9.44am, arriving at the Junction at 10.11am. After a three minute wait, it set off again for Blaenau Ffestiniog, arriving there at 11.16am. It departed for Llandudno Junction at 12/05pm, arriving there at 1/22pm and made a second trip to Blaenau Ffestiniog, departing at 1/45pm and returning from there at 3/10pm before arriving at the Junction at 4/16pm. After parking the unit, the crew travelled home passenger.

The working might not seem out of the ordinary at first glance, but it was unusual in that Llandudno Junction men had not previously worked to Amlwch and did not sign for the road to Afonwen either. Consequently it was necessary to provide a Bangor pilotman for each working. Similarly, whilst Bangor men knew the road to Llandudno Junction, they did not know the Ffestiniog road, and also had to be provided with a pilotman. Despite this new route working, when the DMU's came into regular service, Bangor and Llandudno Junction men kept to their own routes, and the exercise in new route learning proved a waste of time and money.

With the construction of the Nuclear Power station at Trawsfynydd, some heavy electrical equipment which was out of gauge was transported by rail to Blaenau Ffestiniog, and called for very careful work on behalf of the traffic and operating departments. The transformers had to be slewed on their wagons twice during the course of the journey down the branch, including one location inside the Ffestiniog tunnel. Clearance was particularly tight, and the load was 'walked' through the entire length of the tunnel, with engineers checking clearances on either side and headroom clearances. Their calculations had proved correct, although it is on record that at one point, there was less than half an inch to spare whilst half way through the long tunnel.

9. Llandudno Junction. About 1925. Taken from a road overbridge east of the Junction and looking towards Conwy, this view shows LNWR signals with a repeater arm at lower level, behind which can be seen Junction No.1. box. Sighting of the signals was obstructed by the bridge and difficult, hence the height of the posts. In the siding stands Llandudno District coach set No.822 comprising four coaches of six wheel stock. which stood from 11.13am until 3/47pm daily, and the next working of the set along the branch.   *J.M. Dunn.*

BLAENAU FFESTINIOG.

Blaenau Ffestiniog developed as a result of the slate quarrying and mining industry that developed in the second half of the eighteenth century, and lies north of the village of Ffestiniog. The earliest slate quarrying began at Diphwys, the slate being transported down the Vale of Ffestiniog on pannier or by wagon to the quays on the Afon Dwyryd. The marshlands at the mouth of the Glaslyn were drained with the building of embankments and a harbour was established where the river scoured out a deep channel, now known as Porthmadog. The first railway line to Blaenau was proposed to Parliament in 1824 linking the quarries with Portmadoc, and to be known as the Festiniog Railway. There was also a rival proposal, but both Bills were rejected. The successful Festiniog Railway Bill was given the Royal Assent on 25th May 1832 which permitted construction of a narrow gauge line, which opened on 20th April 1836. The line was worked by gravity and horse power, and the impact on Blaenau was to increase output significantly over subsequent years, with a corresponding increase in manpower. By the time the standard gauge line through the Conwy valley reached Blaenau, the industry was approaching its peak output.

The first permanent station at Blaenau consisted of a single wide platform some 160 yards long, on the Up side, which was subsequently extended in the 1950s. A loco release road and two sidings ran parallel to the platform road. The main two storey building was constructed of buff brick with timber cladding, and slate roofing with a canopy which extended over the platform area. The high altitude above sea level ensured that rainfall and adverse weather conditions prevailed for most of the year, which affected the appearance of the buildings and despite regular maintenance, presented a depressing sight, even on sunny days. This became more pronounced following the enforced neglect due to the war, and the structure deteriorated rapidly. The building was demolished in 1951 and replaced by wooden huts, that served for a few years until replaced by a modern single story structure with traditional slate roof about 1956. A combined single locomotive and carriage shed, one and three roads respectively, on the Up side stood north of the platform, with access off the platform road. An internal brick wall separated the two

10. Blaenau Ffestiniog. 11th May 1949. Stanier 2-6-2T No.**40209**, with the enlarged boiler, distinguishable by the separate top feed and dome, runs around the stock off the 12/35pm from Llandudno Junction whilst the fireman stands by the small two lever frame alongside the last coach. The expansive width of the platform is apparant here and the station building, shabby and in need of paint seems to be in fair order. In the yard can be seen additional coaching stock standing on the tranship siding whilst a brake van for the 2/40pm Up freight working stands alongside. *E.S.Russell.*

11. Blaenau Ffestiniog. About 1923. LNWR six wheel stock stands at the platform whilst the station buildings present a clean and tidy appearance. The goods yard is full of stock. In the foreground, the Festiniog Railway buildings seem dwarfed by its standard gauge neighbour. The single Fairlie 0-4-4T *"Taliesin"* stands at the head of a passenger working to the terminus at Duffwys. Note the three narrow gauge four wheel coaches behind the engine. *Photo: Topical Press Agency.*

departments but latterly the south west road of the loco department was out of use before the shed closed following which the track was lifted and the carriage department acquired the remaining road. The locomotive turntable was located off the goods yard access road and a water tank stood near the throat of the goods yard, convenient for locomotives running around the train. A tall signal box stood between the carriage shed and the running line, the lever frame controlling seventeen points and ten signals. Conflicting reasons are given for the height of the box, one being the need to oversee the engine shed and carriage siding roads and the turntable, which was located some distance away. This was replaced by an exposed eighteen lever LNWR tappet frame, of which three levers were spare, off the platform ramp at the north end. A low level box size 14ft x 9ft was erected over the frame about 1938. The box was renamed 'Blaenau Ffestiniog North' by 1954 but this box in turn became redundant and was taken out of use in 1971. The carriage shed was taken out of use before the Second World War, the track removed and the buildings subsequently demolished. Crosville Motor Services built a modern depot, workshop and yard on the site in the early 1960s and vacated their old cramped premises by the Festiniog Railway's Duffws station.

The goods yard was extensive and the standard gauge lines were interspersed with narrow gauge tracks that came off the Festiniog Railway Company's line. A raised tranship platform ran parallel to the passenger platform for much of its length, with standard gauge lines on either side. The narrow gauge lines were at standard gauge wagon floor height, to facilitate easier loading, and avoid breakages in handling. Beyond the tranship platform was a large goods warehouse, with standard and narrow gauge tracks passing through. The yard extended to accommodate a

network of narrow gauge lines, the various Slate Quarries in the district stacking roofing slate on the site. Another nest of sidings provided facilities for other mineral traffic from the standard gauge line. A standard gauge rail wagon weighbridge was located on a siding near the loco turntable road, and another weighbridge for road traffic was located in the yard. A small coal merchant's office stood at the road entrance to the yard. The Goods shed survived intact until the 1980s when it was finally demolished and the site is now used as a parking ground by a private bus operator. The narrow gauge sidings remained in use after the Festiniog Railway closed in 1946 and the various Quarries used their own motive power to bring the wagons into the yard until general traffic ceased on 4th May 1964 when the slate was taken away from the quarries by road. Coal traffic survived until March 1984.

The southern end of the wide platform was used by Crosville buses who effected an interchange with the rail traffic.

When the decision was taken to close the G.W.R. line from Bala and effect a connection with the LNWR line for the removal of the Nuclear waste from Trawsfynydd, the connection was made by removing the narrow gauge tracks and slewing the standard gauge platform road onto the formation. A road and bridge over the course of the old line was rebuilt and connection made with the GWR metals north of the latter station buildings. The road to Tanygrisiau was widened with an access to the Crosville depot. The adjoining F.R. buildings and track were removed about this time, although the formation of the trackbed was retained and subsequently reinstated.

On 22nd March 1982, the new interchange station, on the site of the former GWR station with the Festiniog railway, came into operation, and on the same day the former L.M.R. station closed.

12. Blaenau Ffestiniog. 20th October 1950. (Above). Taken from the buffer stops looking towards Llandudno Junction. The station site is dominated by the slate waste tips which seem to emphasise the run down appearance of the buildings. The tranship sidings and yard are nearly empty although some narrow gauge wagons can be seen beyond the yard crane. A Morris Commercial lorry on the platform is the only indication that the station is still in use although the outline of figures can be seen under the canopy. *British Railways L.M. Region.*

13. Blaenau Ffestiniog. 20th October 1950. (Centre). The run down state of the passenger platform buildings is apparent in this view taken from the tranship sidings. The missing slates on the roof as well as the need for a coat of paint indicate that the building's days are numbered, and this Official view is one of several taken on the same day, perhaps to justify the demolition of the buildings and replacement with something modern. The rain merely heightens the gloom. *British Railways L.M. Region.*

14. Blaenau Ffestiniog. 20th October 1950. The exterior of the passenger building presented an even more dilapidated appearance, heightened by the use of yellow brick in the wet weather. The wooden cladding has come away in places revealing the brickwork underneath. The ornate ventilator over the toilets seems to blend in with the overall appearance. Contrast this view with No. 11 on the previous page when the Railway seemed to take pains to attract customers by keeping its building is reasonable order. Welcome revenue was obtained by the use of advertising hoardings, Astons being a prime contributor in North Wales. *British Railways L.M. Region.*

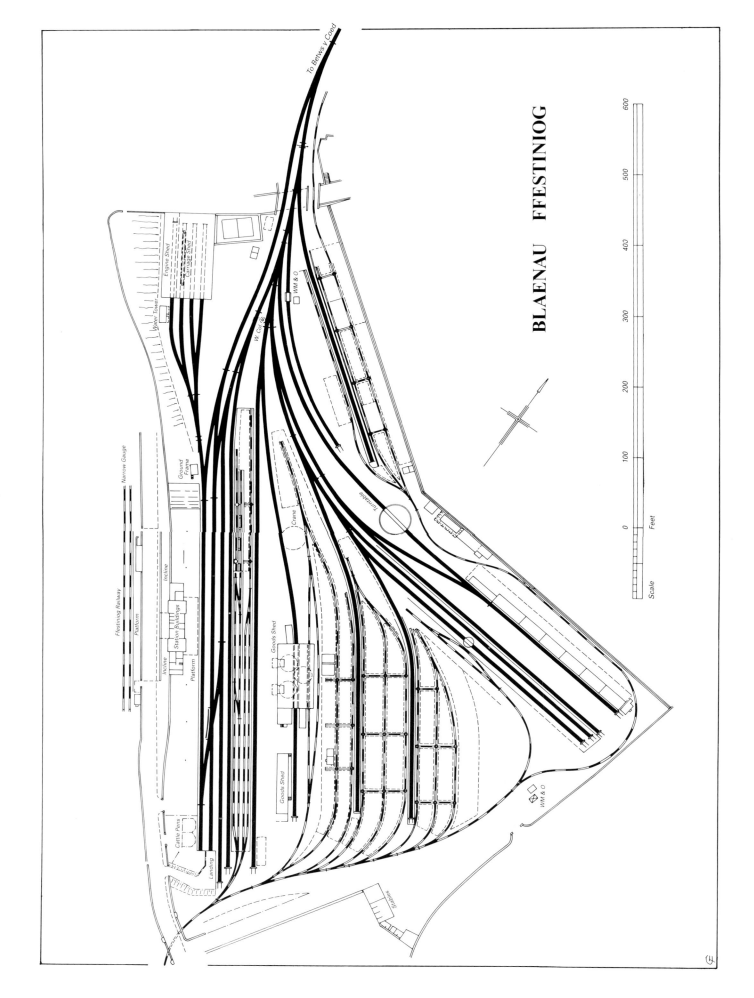

BLAENAU FFESTINIOG

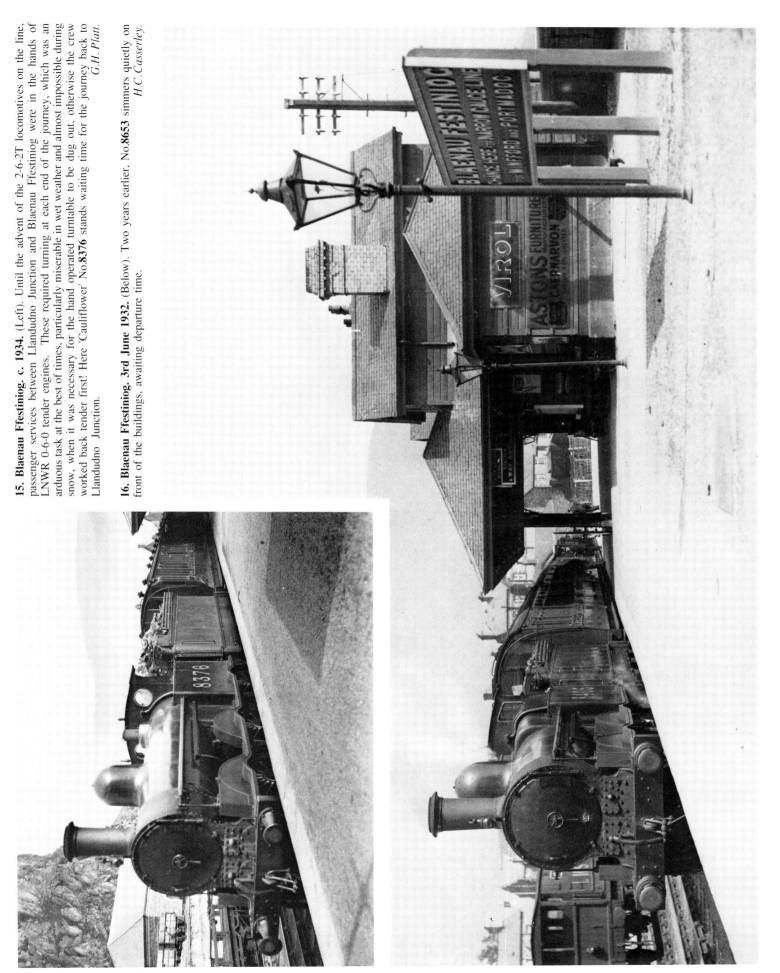

15. Blaenau Ffestiniog. c. 1934. (Left). Until the advent of the 2-6-2T locomotives on the line, passenger services between Llandudno Junction and Blaenau Ffestiniog were in the hands of LNWR 0-6-0 tender engines. These required turning at each end of the journey, which was an arduous task at the best of times, particularly miserable in wet weather and almost impossible during snow, when it was necessary for the hand operated turntable to be dug out, otherwise the crew worked back tender first! Here 'Cauliflower' No.**8376** stands waiting time for the journey back to Llandudno Junction.

G.H. Platt.

16. Blaenau Ffestiniog. 3rd June 1932. (Below). Two years earlier, No.**8653** simmers quietly on front of the buildings, awaiting departure time.

H.C. Casserley.

17. Blaenau Ffestiniog. 7th August 1948. (Top) Stanier 2-6-2T No.**40209** ofLlandudno Junction [7A] shed stands awaiting departure time with the 7/55pm to Llandudno. The locomotive one of the first of its class to be renumbered by British Railways. There were six members of the class at 7A, all working on the Conwy Valley line. The yard is somewhat bare, and by this date, most slate products were despatched from the quarry by road transport, although the yard was still used for stacking and sorting slate

W.A.Camwell.

18. Blaenau Ffestiniog 1938. (Centre Right). 2-6-2T No.**105** stands at the platform after working a morning turn from Llandudno. The stock sets used on the line on regular workings were all non corridor coaches and seldom strayed of their diagrams. There are some narrow and standard gauge wagons in the yard, just visible behind the engine.

Collection: Bill Rear.

19. Blaenau Ffestiniog. 1952. (Lower Right). Stanier 2-6-2T No.**40083** coasts into the platform and past the small signal cabin with the 3/05pm from Llandudno. The narrow gauge sidings just visible behind the locomotive are full of empty LNWR built narrow gauge slate wagons constructed in anticipation of persuading the quarry owners to divert traffic via their route. They were only partially successful and until the outbreak of the Second World War, most slate was sent over the Festiniog Railway to Porthmadoc. The signal box was an adaptation of the small portable buildings originated by F.W. Webb and used widely for use such as waiting rooms, small goods sheds etc.

J.W.T. House.

20. Blaenau Ffestiniog. c.1922. The slate quarries relied heavily on the railways not only to carry their goods to the customers, but also to store the graded slate in their yards. Note the neat stacks of dressed slate which occupied every available space. The sign proclaims this to be "Oakeley Quarries Slate Wharf". A fascinating collection of pre grouping wagons including G.C., L.& Y., L.N.W.R., M.R. and G.N.R. as well as a Private Owner wagon are visible.

Topical Press Agency.

21. Blaenau Ffestiniog. 12th October 1951. (Centre Left) The LNWR 'Cauliflower' 0-6-0 had been replaced on the passenger turns on the line, but still worked the goods turns. Here **58365** waits in the yard after turning prior to working back to Llandudno Junction. *D.H. Ballantyne.*

22. Blaenau Ffestiniog, 16th July 1964. (Left). Ivatt 2-6-2T No.**41244** draws up to the water tank after working the morning freight from Llandudno Junction. The small signal cabin has been replaced and relocated and is no longer at the platform ramp. The new Crosville depot gleams alongside, built on the site of the former Loco and Carriage shed. These small 2-6-2Ts had the monopoly of services over the branch until the passenger turns were lost to the D.M.U.s in 1956. They still performed regularly on the freight turns almost to the end of steam in North Wales. *C.L. Caddy.*

23. Blaenau Ffestiniog. 1964.
The ramshackle buildings were demolished and temporarily replaced by a wooden hut in the early 1950s. A much smaller but functional permanent single storey building was constructed which served until the new interchange station was opened in 1982. The wide platform remained and until the link to the former GWR line was installed, the track and platform ran parallel to the sidings ending in buffer stops.
British Railways L.M.Region.

24. Blaenau Ffestiniog. 1964.
The exterior of the replacement station building, seen from the site of the Festiniog Railway platform, which had been removed when the link line was installed under the necessary road alterations. The wall protecting the road access ramp was retained, and blended in with the modern structure. The small loading bay for parcel traffic is in stark contrast to the lavish facilities that were once provided.
British Railways L.M.Region.

25. Blaenau Ffestiniog. 16th July 1964. The alterations brought about by the new connecting link line become evident in this view. The platform has been cut back and the platform modified to accommodate the track realignment. The goods shed is in the process of being demolished whilst beyond the station, the new Crosville bus garage and workshop stand on the site of the former Loco and Carriage Shed. *C.L. Caddy.*

26. Blaenau Ffestiniog. 1956.
The regular passenger service to Blaenau Ffestiniog was taken over completely by DMUs from March of that year, and only the freight traffic remained steam hauled. Nevertheless excursion and special charter trains were steam hauled, and supporters of the local football team regularly chartered trains to take them to away matches. Stanier 2-6-2T No.**40133** is seen here running around the three coach non corridor set prior to working W354A to Llandudno. The DMU had to vacate the platform temporarily and Derby Lightweight Power Car No.M79143 and trailer is seen here in one of the storage sidings. The temporary wooden station buildings are just visible behind the crowd of supporters. *W.A. Camwell.*

27.   Blaenau Ffestiniog. 1956.
The station platform was conveniently situated to effect road to rail transfers, and Crosville buses met most trains. The DMU seen above has now reverted to the platform road, and has loaded up to capacity. In the foreground, Leyland TD4 of 1936, No. M.509, which Crosville acquired from Sheffield Corporation in 1946 stands awaiting departure time on service 528 for Pwllheli. The bus survived until 1958 when the chassis was sold for scrap. At the time of this picture, it had been rebodied for the second time, and the body was transferred to another vehicle on withdrawal.
W.A. Camwell.

28. Blaenau Ffestiniog. 1958. Another view of the interchange facilities at the station. This view shows the platform before the track realignment took place to connect with the former GWR line. In the background can be seen the North Western Hotel, once railway owned. In the foreground can be seen the small two lever frame which controlled the release road point. On the platform can be seen Bristol LL5G Fleet No. SLG 160 working the Tanygrisiau to Ffestiniog 'swinger' whilst an unidentified double decker waits in the background, probably working the Blaenau Ffestiniog to Pwllheli service. During the period that the Festiniog Railway operated only as far as Tan y Bwlch, much was made of this rail/bus interchange facility to provide a round trip excursion. Buses were also laid on to take interested parties to the nearby Stwlan dam. *C.L. Caddy.*

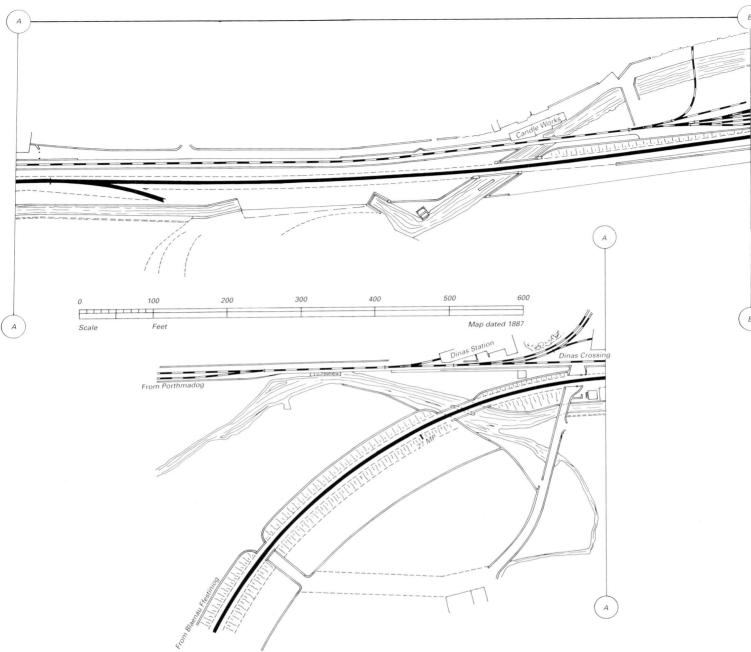

Map dated 1887

Scale   Feet

0   100   200   300   400   500   600

Candle Works

Dinas Station   Dinas Crossing

From Porthmadog

27 MP

From Blaenau Ffestiniog

29. Blaenau Ffestiniog. The entrance and portal at the south end of Blaenau Ffestiniog, is crowned by a large stone panel bearing the name of the engineer W. Smith, and the date, 1879, when the last section of the line finally opened. The tunnel carries the line through the solid rock of Moel Dyrnogydd at almost 800 feet above sea level. At 2 miles 206 yards in length, it is the eighth longest tunnel in the country. Until closure of Greaves Siding in the 1960's, it was virtually impossible to shunt without the locomotive spending much of the time inside the tunnel.

G. H. Platt.

44. Dolwyddelan. 1949. A fine view, showing the individual design of the island platform. The extended roof over the platforms tends to dominate the station although the protection it afforded passengers was surely welcome. The coal siding was in the foreground, the local merchant usually receiving two wagons a week, which he bagged, weighed and distributed from the yard. The lever frame was slightly raised above platform height as can be seen in this view.
Derek Chaplin.

45. Dolwyddelan. 1949. A close up view of the eighteen lever frame mounted on the platform before it was enclosed. At the time of this photograph, thirteen levers were in use, with spaces for a further five. Up and Down line 'Train on Line' indicators were mounted on the gable wall, as was the Lever Frame Diagram and an enclosed oil lamp. The single line token equipment was installed in the station office. Railway employees gather around the Down platform, close to where they can put their tools in the guards van whilst an Up train stands in the platform awaiting the arrival of the train to Blaenau Ffestiniog. *Derek Chaplin.*

46. Dolwyddelan. 1959. Taken from the Llandudno Junction end of the Up platform and looking towards Blaenau Ffestiniog, this view shows the replacement Goods Shed, with its small loading platform which replaced the large goods shed. The loop line which passed through the latter building was removed, and the remaining line realigned, continuing on to the coal siding. The weigh office can be seen centre right. *W.G.Rear.*

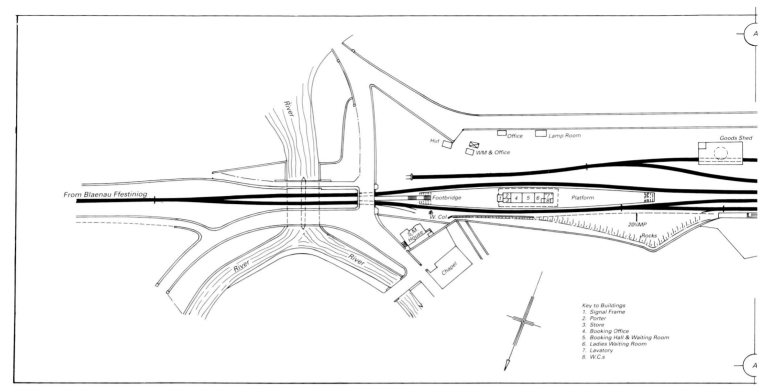

Key to Buildings
1. Signal Frame
2. Porter
3. Store
4. Booking Office
5. Booking Hall & Waiting Room
6. Ladies Waiting Room
7. Lavatory
8. W.C.s

47. Dolwyddelan. March 1956. The replacement of steam hauled services by DMUs was at a time when traffic on the line was at its most intensive and many workings crossed trains at one or more points on the line. Seen here is the 3.52pm from Llandudno Junction to Blaenau Ffestiniog which had crossed Up direction DMUs at Llanrwst and here at Dolwyddelan, where it met the 4.25pm from Blaenau to Llandudno. Behind the Llandudno train the Goods Shed can be seen, shortly to be demolished. *W.A. Camwell.*

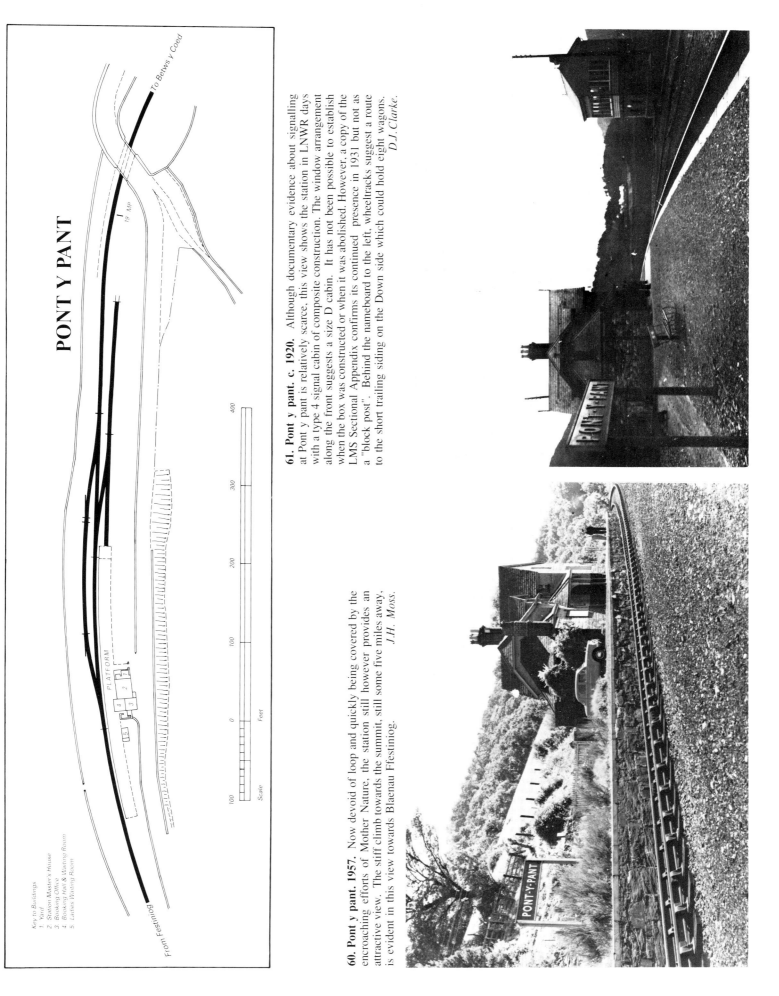

PONT Y PANT

Key to Buildings
1. Yard
2. Station Master's House
3. Booking Office
4. Booking Hall & Waiting Room
5. Ladies Waiting Room

To Betws y Coed

19 MP

PLATFORM

From Festiniog

Scale   Feet

100   0   100   200   300   400

61. Pont y pant. c. 1920. Although documentary evidence about signalling at Pont y pant is relatively scarce, this view shows the station in LNWR days with a type 4 signal cabin of composite construction. The window arrangement along the front suggests a size D cabin. It has not been possible to establish when the box was constructed or when it was abolished. However, a copy of the LMS Sectional Appendix confirms its continued presence in 1931 but not as a "block post". Behind the nameboard to the left, wheeltracks suggest a route to the short trailing siding on the Down side which could hold eight wagons.
D.J. Clarke.

60. Pont y pant. 1957. Now devoid of loop and quickly being covered by the encroaching efforts of Mother Nature, the station still however provides an attractive view. The stiff climb towards the summit, still some five miles away, is evident in this view towards Blaenau Ffestiniog.
J.H. Moss.

62. Lledr Valley. September 1938.
Taken from a Down train in a rocky cutting between Betws y Coed and Pont y pant. LNWR 'Coal Tank' engines worked through to Blaenau less frequently than tender engines. An explanation offered by Llandudno Junction staff was that the turntable at Blaenau was under repair about this time, and it was not considered desireable to run tender engines in reverse for the twenty seven mile journey. No doubt the train crew would agree, especially if the weather was poor.   *J.M. Dunn.*

63. Lledr Valley. 1954. Ivatt 2-6-2T No.**41236** heads a three coach local to Blaenau Ffestiniog, passing through the Lledr valley at the point where the railway clings to the hillside, keeping the river close company. These engines were masters of the job and despite the gradient of 1 in 47 steamed freely as shown in this view. They were preferred to the Class 3 Stanier 2-6-2T they replaced, and were considered to be more powerful. This view provides a good example of what the LNWR described as "Dry Rubble Breast Walling", in other words, the stone walls. They were to be built with a face batter (sloping face) and not to be less than two feet wide at the top. They were indeed built to last as this view shows, eighty years on.   *H. Rogers Jones.*

64. Gethin's Bridge. This structure was colloquially named after Owen Gethin Jones, a stonemason of Penmachno, and the sub-contractor to the main Contractors D. & E. Jones, of Betws y Coed. It is he who was responsible for the masonry on the stations and bridges, and this, his best known work being officially titled as "Lledr Viaduct". It comprised seven stone arches. The Railway Inspector, Colonel Rich, commenting in his Official Report, was not happy with the quality of masonry, and preferring 'good rustic rubble work, with fitted joints, filled with mortar, toned to the proper colour...', but despite this observation, the work was passed. This view shows the main span. *J.M. Dunn.*

65. Gethin's Bridge. March 1956. An unusual view of the bridge, showing one of the newly introduced DMUs on a working to Blaenau Ffestiniog. The main road from Betws y Coed to Blaenau Ffestiniog skirts the forestry plantation in the distance.
W.A. Camwell.

66. Gethin's Bridge. 1956. Another view of the main span of the bridge, with a Blaenau bound DMU crossing the span. Note the castellated refuges on either side and end of the bridge, and the harmonious way which the structure blends into the landscape. The bridge was numbered 34 on the line, its seven arches being made up of five with a span of 30 feet - the first being skew,. one with an opening of 80 feet - over the River Lledr, and one an occupation arch of 9 feet at the Blaenau end. It was built as part of the No.1. contract and it is interesting to note that the original specification called for nine openings. Local materials were to be used where possible, but the LNWR specifically requested Penmaenmawr stone for the quoins, strings and copings". *H. Rogers Jones.*

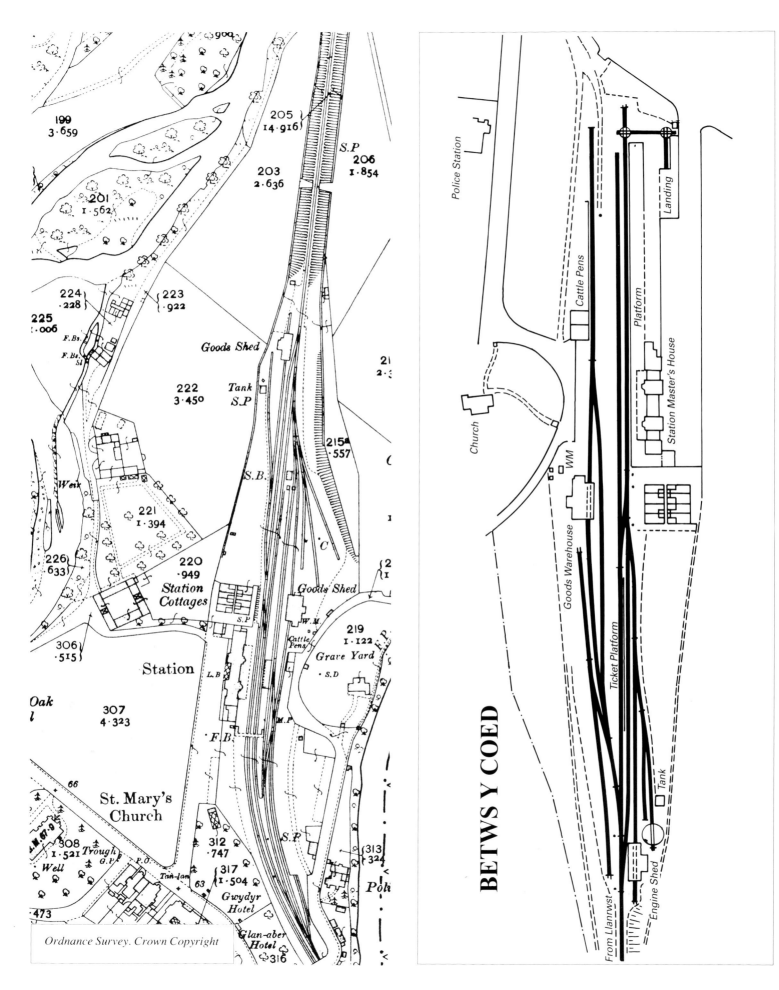

Ordnance Survey. Crown Copyright

199
3·659

205
14·916

201
1·562

203
2·636

206
1·854

S.P

224
·228

223
·922

225
·006

F.Bs.

F.Bs.
Sl.

Goods Shed

222
3·450

Tank
S.P

215
·557

21
2·3

Weir

S.B.

221
1·394

226
·633

220
·949

Station
Cottages

S.P

Goods Shed

C

W.M.

219
1·122

306
·515

Station

L.B

Cattle
Pens

Grave Yard

· S.D

Oak
l

307
4·323

F.B.

M.P.

66

St. Mary's
Church

308
1·521

Trough
G.P.

P.O.

312
·747

S.P

313
·324

Well

Tan-lan

63

317
1·504

Pol

·473

Gwydyr
Hotel

Glan-aber
Hotel

316

BETWS Y COED

Police Station

Church

Cattle Pens

Landing

Platform

Station Master's House

WM

Goods Warehouse

Ticket Platform

Tank

From Llanrwst

Engine Shed

BETWS Y COED

Fifteen miles from Llandudno Junction and the largest intermediate station on the line, Betws y Coed was at the commencement of the almost continuous climb to Blaenau Ffestiniog, and which taxed engines and the skills of the drivers and firemen alike.

The line was opened from Llanrwst to Betws for freight traffic in October 1867 and for passengers the following April. A drawing in the possession of Mr Alan Pratt, who founded the Conwy Valley Museum located in the Goods Yard on the Down side, shows a single platform considerably shorter and straight. The track ended at buffer stops, with a wagon turntable located at the platform ramp. This led to a short length of track at right angles to the running line, and another wagon turntable which gave siding access to a landing dock. The Goods warehouse was in the yard on the Down side, whilst north of the platform on the Up side was an engine shed, with siding and turntable road. The drawing is reproduced opposite. It will be noticed that there was a ticket platform before the station was reached, a common feature to many LNWR locations. The drawing shows the positions of five signal posts but no signal box is marked.

The Station building was a lavish structure, as may be seen from the photographs, and the Station Master had accommodation on the first floor. There were eight cottages for employees on the Up side just beyond the station ramp. A large canopy covered the platform area, giving shelter to passengers.

When the line was extended to Blaenau, the track was realigned to pass under a new road bridge that gave access to the Goods Yard, Police Station and the Church. The Up passenger platform was thus extended, with the wagon turntables and loading dock removed. The new loading dock being located on the Down side at the Blaenau end and off the Goods loop to a short spur on the slate wharf. Siding capacity in the Goods Yard was increased and a yard crane was installed. A signal cabin was located at the Llanrwst end of the Down side, just off the platform. A second, small, cabin was located at the southern end just beyond the road overbridge (No.25) at the commencement of the line to Pont y pant. This controlled access to the goods yard and could release a train staff for trains proceeding south. The Down platform was installed in July 1898 and included a shelter for passengers. It was a fairly basic structure, although the canopy extended to the platform edge. The two platforms were connected by a footbridge (24A), which was enclosed, the covering of which was removed when the loop was taken out.

The main station building less canopy, and the cottages survive to the present day, although the former is now a restaurant. The goods yard is occupied by the Conwy Valley Museum complex. The engine shed was demolished before the Second World War although the siding and inspection pit remained until the 1980s.

67. Betws y Coed. 11th May 1949. Stanier 2-6-2T No.**40133** of Llandudno Junction shed stands at the Down platform with the 10.33am from Llandudno Junction to Blaenau Ffestiniog, the fireman building up his fire in readiness for eleven miles of unremitting slog with a class of engine reputed to be indifferent performers. The platforms were extended when the station was altered in 1898. *E.S. Russell.*

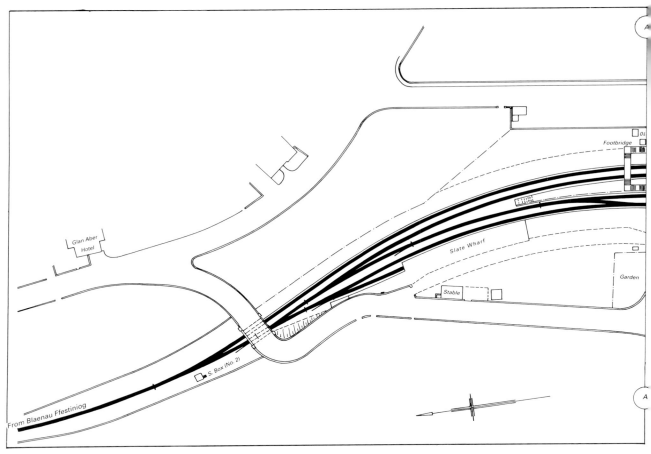

Glan Aber Hotel

Footbridge

Slate Wharf

Garden

Stable

S. Box (No. 2)

From Blaenau Ffestiniog

68. Betws y Coed. 1956. A new Derby Lightweight DMU glides smoothly away from the Down platform and round the sharp curve before gaining the single line to Dolwyddelan. The track from the Goods Yard joins the Down line and a Camping Coach stands alongside the now disused slate quay, which was for end loading only. Beyond the Camping Coach can be seen the Down platform shelter, which contrasts strongly with the expansive Up side buildings. Note also the difference in platform lengths.   *H. Rogers Jones.*

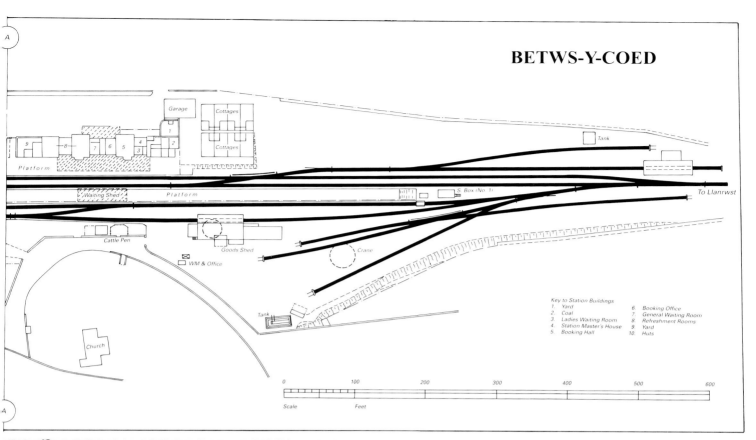

BETWS-Y-COED

Key to Station Buildings
1. Yard
2. Coal
3. Ladies Waiting Room
4. Station Master's House
5. Booking Hall
6. Booking Office
7. General Waiting Room
8. Refreshment Rooms
9. Yard
10. Huts

69. Betws y Coed. 1957. This view gives some idea of the contrast between the Up and Down platform buildings. Notice how the canopies extend to give protection for the passengers. Beyond the water tank is the Up starter. The signal box stands at the northern entrance to the Goods Yard. The footbridge was built up of standard components and supported on rolled wrought iron columns. The large numbers of seasonal visitors resulted in wider than normal footways which were protected from the elements by a glazed covering.

J.H. Moss.

70. Betws y Coed. 1960. Taken from the Blaenau end of the Down platform, the expanse of the Up platform seems hard to justify when most trains in steam days consisted of two or three coaches. The goods yard was by this time little used, and a baulk of timber has been placed over the line by the catch point. Beyond the bridge but hidden from view is the small signal cabin which controlled access to the Goods Yard and the merging of the Up and Down loop lines. *W.G.Rear.*

71. Betws y Coed. 1964. The small No.2. Signal Cabin located at the south end of the station, taken from the road overbridge. This box was only 10' 0" by 8' 0" and housed an LNW 18 lever frame of which Lever Nos 1, 3, 11, 12, 13, 14 and 18 were spare.

W.G. Rear.

2nd-SINGLE SINGLE-2nd
BETWS-Y-COED TO
Betws-Y-Coed
Llanrwst &
Trefriw
Betws-Y-Coed
Llanrwst &
Trefriw
8546
LLANRWST & TREFRIW
(M) 1/0 Fare 1/0 (M)
For conditions see over   For conditions see over

72. Betws y Coed. 12th July 1965. Ivatt 2-6-2T No.**41233** of Llandudno Junction shed pulls into the Up platform with the daily freight and draws towards the Up Starter. The daily freight was the only regular steam working on the line. The Water tank has by now been removed from the Up platform although the rest of the station is intact if a little unkempt. A solitary trolley stands on the Down platform. *C.L. Caddy.*

84. Betws y Coed. 1957. (Above). All that remained of the former Engine Shed building for many years was this store that was built into the shed wall. In the foreground is the track from the Down loop to the goods yard, protected by the catch point. Note the miniature arm of the ground signal by the point rodding and signal wires from the No.1. box. A weighted hand operated point lever controls the line to one of the sidings by the yard crane in the yard. *J.H. Moss.*

85. Betws y Coed. 1964. (Centre-left). The gable end of the Goods Shed, showing the small office and the flight of steps leading from the yard. Even though the structure was assembled with local materials, many of the features were inherent with LNWR practice. *W.G. Rear.*

86. Betws y Coed. 1964. (Lower-left). The road approach to the Goods Shed, showing the extension covering the loading ramp. The corrugated sheet extension was used as a grain store, and similar examples were found in many goods yards in North Wales. The yard was only used by coal merchants by this date, and their stocks were dumped against the shed for partial protection against the elements. *W.G. Rear.*

87. Betws y Coed. 11th May 1949. (Above). Stanier 2-6-2T No. **40209,** with the larger 6A boiler and separate top feed, runs into Betws y Coed station with the 12 35pm Llandudno Junction to Blaenau Ffestiniog train. The first coach is a 50ft seven compartment vehicle and almost vintage stock. Note the rectangular water tank in the former loco yard on the far side of the track whilst the lines leading to the Goods Yard branch off the Down loop. *E.S. Russell.*

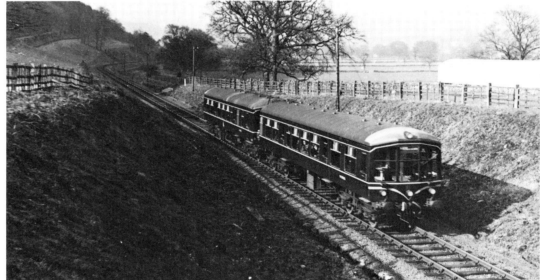

88. Betws y Coed. 1956. (Centre). The gradients on the line between Llandudno Junction and Betws y Coed were relatively gentle and the line passed through pleasant rural agricultural land. A Derby lightweight DMU approaches Betws y Coed on the western side of the valley, heading for Blaenau Ffestiniog, shortly after their introduction to the line. *H. Rogers Jones.*

89. Betws y Coed. 1956. (Lower right). A Derby lightweight DMU crosses over the river Conwy between Llanrwst and Betws y Coed in early spring, shortly after the steam workings were replaced. The river bank shows signs of erosion, and periodically the valley becomes flooded, and at times the services are disrupted. The river constantly posed a threat to the railway at numerous locations and the erosion to the banks in this picture illustrates the problem. This point was, and is, particularly susceptible, the land spans of the bridge (No.20) providing openings to help ease any likely problems caused by a swollen river. *H. Rogers Jones.*

LLANRWST & TREFRIW

The line to Llanrwst was authorised under the Conway & Llanrwst Railway Act of 23rd July 1860. The station was formally opened on 16th June 1863, and public services commenced the following day. The line was transferred to the L.& N.W.R. the following month.

The first station, which was the southern terminus of the single track branch, was located in what subsequently became the goods yard. With the construction of the extension to Betws y Coed, the new line left the Conway & Llanrwst line about 200 yards north of the first station, and a new station was built south of the junction. This consisted of a single platform with passing loop and buildings on the Up side. The Down platform was added later, a stone built shelter with overhanging slate roof, and waiting rooms at each end separated by an open area. The footbridge was a later addition. The main building and goods shed are constructed of local stone, with slate roofs. The windows and doors are faced with dressed stone. The station building is a large structure, with the usual offices provided.

A carriage landing was located at the Llandudno Junction end of the Up platform with road access through the goods yard.

The goods yard was located on the Up side of the line with access north of the passenger platforms off the Up loop line. The yard consisted of four sidings with two tracks on either side of a "V" formation with the apex near the signal box at the north end of the site running into a shunting neck. One road passed through the goods shed with a second running parallel and outside the shed. The outer of the second pair of lines in the yard ran alongside cattle loading pens. The Railway Clearing House publication *"Handbook of Railway Stations 1929"* listed the crane power in the yard as of 10 ton capacity.

The signal box was parallel to the Up loop line and was size 16' 2$\frac{1}{2}$" x 12' 0" mounted on a brick base. The elevation was 8' 0" and was located 6' 0" from the Up loop line. The frame was an LNW Tappet type set of 20 levers of which levers 5, 10 and 13 were spare and 4 and 16 were spaces. The box remained in commission until very recently, although it merely served as a token exchange point and controlled the passing loop. The single line token equipment was located in the box, and the sections north were to Tal y Cafn, which had been taken out of service by 1964, the section being extended to Llandudno Junction. In the opposite direction, the section to Betws y Coed was lengthened to Blaenau Ffestiniog, eliminating Betws y Coed and Dolwyddelan as token exchange points. The footbridge had been removed by 1982. In 1989 a new platform with the name of Llanrwst was opened 40 chains south on the Down side immediately beyond the 85 yard Llanrwst tunnel. This is more centrally located for the town but the former station remains in service and is now renamed "Llanrwst North". The passing loop remains in position but is rarely used.

90. Llanrwst. 1957. View towards Llandudno Junction from the "Plas Isaf" road overbridge south of the station. *J.H. Moss.*

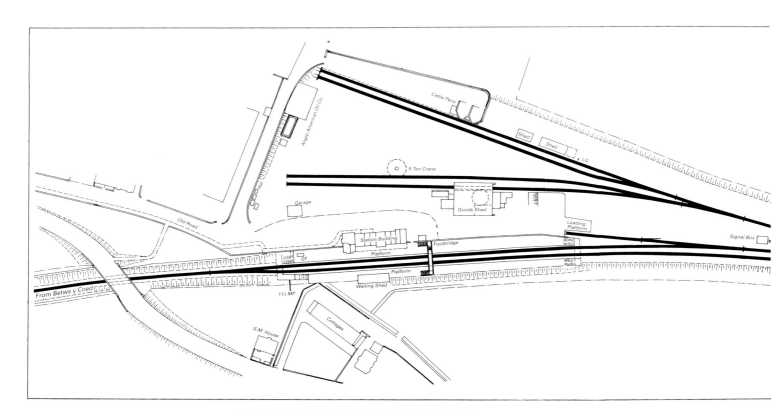

91. Llanwst & Trefriw. 1964. The commencement of the single line to Betws y Coed. At the time of this photograph the footbridge was still in use and the warning signs advising the public not to cross the line on the trolley walkway still applied. Notice the very tall signal beyond the road overbridge and the gas lamps on either platform. *W.G. Rear*.

92. Llanrwst & Trefriw. 5th July 1963. The main building on the Up platform, photographed from a Blaenau bound train. The totem on the gas lamp gives the station its full title, whilst the larger nameboard on the gable end omits 'Trefriw'. Over the wall can be seen covered vans in the goods yard. Notice also the ornate chimney breast and pots. By the canopy can be seen portable steps, which were necessary because of the low height of the platform. The station staff have made efforts to keep the station tidy, and the flower bed edging stones have been picked out with whitewash.

J.J.Davis.

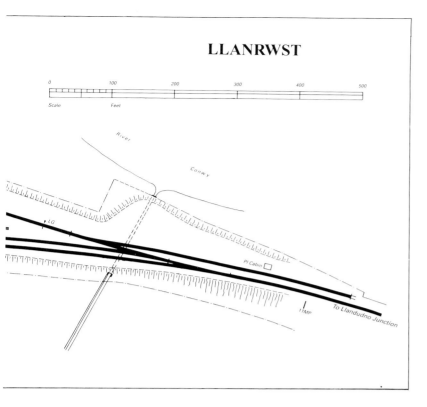

LLANRWST

Scale   Feet
0   100   200   300   400   500

River
Conwy

LG
Pl Cabin
11MP
To Llandudno Junction

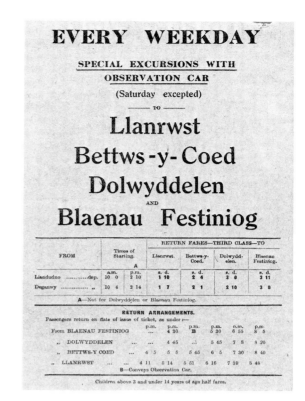

93. Llanrwst & Trefriw. September 1938. ex LNWR 0-6-0 'Cauliflower' No.**8608** pulls into Llanrwst station with an Up working. The Observation Car is located immediately behind the engine and which was attached to the trailing end of Down trains. The working is probably the 4.30pm from Blaenau Ffestiniog to Llandudno. Two Observation Cars worked on the branch daily in the summer season, each one containing a guide who gave a commentary on the attractions and sights visible from the coach. A third coach worked from Rhyl to Llanberis and return.

G.H. Platt.

94. Llanrwst & Trefriw. The exterior of the main building on the Up side presented a rather austere appearance with the closest portion of the building reminiscent of a Chapel, apart from the ornamental chimney stack. The goods shed and office stand on the site of the first station when the line terminated here. A solitary lorry stands by the road loading bay, although normally two lorries were based here and daily worked the L.M.S. Country Lorry Services. Despite the absence of signs of life, the station was generally busy and the Goods Yard was very active.

W.A. Camwell.

95. Llanrwst & Trefriw. 1956. A general view of the station, taken from the Down platform. A Blaenau bound DMU stands at the platform, the station staff loading freight into the Guard's compartment from the barrow. Two passenger crosses the footbridge whilst others make their way to the exit on the Up platform. Notice the extent of the paved area of the Down platform. *W.A. Camwell*

96. Llanrwst & Trefriw. The main buildings on the Up platform in L.N.W.R. days. On the extreme left can be seen the large station nameboard, whilst a variety of sack trucks, hand carts and barrows rest under the canopy. The dial of a weighing machine gleams in the shade. The track is covered with ash ballast above the sleeper level but it is difficult to establish why some sections have been cleared beneath the rail, close inspection revealing that it is not because of rail ends/fishplates.. Notice also the low height of the platform, which necessitated the provision of steps for passengers. *D.J. Clarke collection.*

97. Llanrwst & Trefriw. 1964. The Down platform shelter, viewed from the footbridge.The overhanging roof is intended to give passengers protection from the elements at times when the small covered centre area became full. Notice the portable steps under the gable end window with another set at the Betws y Coed end. The fencing had been painted although recent growth tended to conceal it. *W.G. Rear.*

98. Llanrwst & Trefriw. 1964. Taken from the Up platform looking towards Llandudno Junction, this view shows the open footbridge with the gas lamps mounted at each end. In the distance can be seen the signal cabin, whilst a four car DMU departs for Llandudno. A porter makes his way to the cabin with the train staff token.   *W.G. Rear.*

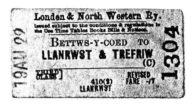

99. Llanrwst & Trefriw. 1964. (Centre-upper). Taken from the Goods Yard looking towards the neck. Coal wagons line the No.4. siding whilst box vans stand alongside in No.3. road. The corner of the Goods Shed blocks the view of the carriage landing. The signal cabin can be seen in the distance. There was a considerable amount of freight traffic, mainly agricultural produce, grain and livestock, to and from Llanrwst until the service was closed to all but coal, and this was discontinued very shortly afterwards, although the local coal merchant continued to use the yard after the removal of the sidings. The small building to the left of the goods shed was a small timber framed portable store. The side walls were asbestos sheeting, the whole being erected on a frame of recovered sleepers. Largest users of the facility were Silcocks, the agricultural foodstuffs merchants.   *W.G. Rear.*

100. Llanrwst & Trefriw. 1964. (Centre-lower)The two bay Goods shed dealt with a considerable volume of traffic in its heyday, and the building was used to store grain and animal feedstuffs which were distributed from the yard by the Railway's own lorries. Behind the open wagon can be seen the yard crane, and mineral wagons fill the sidings beyond. The small office in front of the shed was used by the local corn merchant.   *W.G. Rear.*

101. Llanrwst & Trefriw. 1964. (Lower). Accommodation for some freight traffic was very limited in the goods department and this 50ft full brake body was brought in to remedy the situation. It was parted from its chassis and mounted on concrete blocks. It is not known when it was installed, but it is understood that it was after the Second World War.
    W.G. Rear.

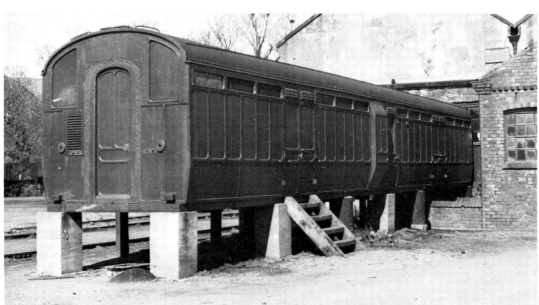

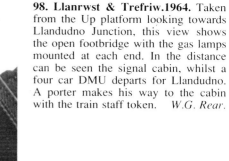

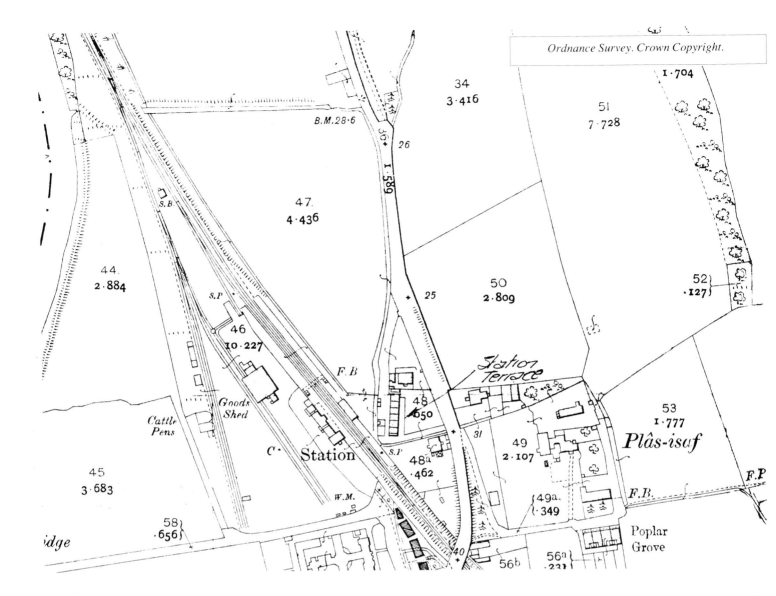

102. Llanrwst & Trefriw. April 1963. 4-6-0 Class 5 No.**45348** of 6G stands at the neck of the Goods Yard at the head of a Class K freight awaiting the road. The guard and fireman stand on the steps talking to the signalman. Notice the bell suspended from the gable end of the cabin whilst the single line token equipment can be seen silhouetted against the window. In the foreground can be seen the bunker with fine chippings, a pair of platelayer's trolley wheels and some large lumps of coal that probably fell off the tender!. The signalman's bike rests under the stairs, ready for the end of the shift. This single freight working had spent one minute over the hour at Llanrwst and would depart at 3.36pm, making its way back to Llandudno Junction. Having left the Junction at 6.30am that morning, the outward working arrived in Blaenau at 10.45am, longest spells of shunting being at Llanrwst and Betws y Coed. Before working up the line, a short return trip was made to Greaves Siding. *Brian Cowlishaw.*

DOLGARROG

It was the topography of the district that led to the development of modern Dolgarrog in the late nineteenth century, when the abundant supply of water created the necessary conditions to harness it as a power source. The Llandudno Improvement Commissioners established a dam, completed in 1881, to enable it to be used for the town's water supply, but it was the possibility of using abundant rainfall of the Carneddau, together with the precipitous drop in terrain immediately behind the present village, as a source for generating electricity that earmarked the area for development. John Robert Gethin Jones, the son of the Mason, Owen Gethin Jones, who built the Lledr Viaduct south of Betws y Coed, and his brother-in-law W.J. Roberts, who bought the old Porth Llwyd Mill, its water rights and some cottages, and another farm, which they subsequently sold a half share interest and with their new partners, set up Gwalia Ltd, that eventually developed the hydro electric plant. Details of this development can be read in Gwynedd Archives "*Dolgarrog An Industrial History*" by Eric Jones & David Gwyn. It was the development of Aluminium which required quantities of electric power for its manufacture that introduced the Aluminium Corporation to Dolgarrog.

In May 1907 an application was made to the Light Railway Commissioners for permission to build a standard gauge line linking the Works with the LNWR which ran on the opposite side of the valley. The scheme was shelved due to a change of policy. Other schemes for a narrow gauge line were proposed and considered but it was the outbreak of World War One that finally created a rail link with the L.N.W.R. and by 1916 a standard gauge siding and connection with the Conwy Valley line was effected and materials could be received from and dispatched to their destinations without transhipping them. A free rail passenger service connected with the LNWR trains to and from the works, which survived until about 1932. The halt opened to the public on 1st February 1917, closed to passengers in 1964 and reopened again on 14th June 1965. The rail connection to the works fell out of use by 1960 and was lifted in 1963, the rail and sleepers being acquired by the Welsh Highland Railway (1964) Ltd and transported to Beddgelert.

The halt consisted of a single wooden platform on the Down side of the line, with two small huts providing the only shelter, together with a couple of name boards and some electric lights. The platform itself was of timber construction and a handrail ran its entire length. A loop on the Up side north of the platform was controlled by a ground frame at either end and locked by the train staff. This loop also gave access to the Aluminium Corporation line.

103. Dolgarrog. 1956. The platform on the Down side was a bleak place to await a train with very little shelter for the passengers in inclement weather. There was a waiting room, located half way along the platform, but it was a little more than a wind break, and the small stove inside did not generate much heat. The structure at the Blaenau end of the platform was a small office, and only staffed for part of the day. A seat, a couple of nameboards and some electric lights completed the inventory. A hand operated level crossing over a minor road was the main reason for providing a presence here. A new DMU approaches the halt on a Blaenau working, and will have one person boarding, although it is likely that the passenger is a Railway employee. Frequently, no one alighted or boarded, although the Local Authority decided that it justified reopening after the initial closure in 1964.
W.A. Camwell.

104. Dolgarrog. 13th July 1966. When the halt was closed in 1964, the buildings and lamps were removed. A year later it reopened, but there was no attempt made to reinstate the shelter although the nameboards and some of the lamps were brought back into use. A telephone was provided for road vehicles that wished to cross the line, and which eliminated the need for a staff presence. Guards issued and collected tickets on the train. Today, all trains call at the halt. *C.L. Caddy.*

105. Between Tal y Cafn & Dolgarrog. 5th July 1904. On this day, LNWR 4' 6" 2-4-2T engine No.**891** and its train of six-wheel coaches, working the 10.25am from Llandudno to Betws y Coed, ran off the rails two miles south of Tal y Cafn and dragged with it the seven coaches, all of which overturned in the process. Fortunately, due to bad weather, there were only six passengers on the train and none of them were injured. The driver, Charles Jones, of Llandudno Junction shed, was badly injured but subsequently recovered to work again. His fireman, John Williams, was scalded and suffered from shock. The engine was turned completely round in the accident. A fortnight later it required eight engines to drag No.**891** free. The enquiry that followed showed that this train (and others in both directions) were timed to cover the six miles in eight minutes, which necessitated speeds of up to 60 mph. The timings were relaxed the following September.

J.M.Dunn collection.

106. Between Tal y Cafn & Dolgarrog. 1953. Stanier 2-6-2T No.**40133**, working the 12.30pm from Llandudno Junction, heads up the valley, keeping the river company. Three coaches was the most that these locomotives could manage successfully without jeopardising water capacity, and the winter months saw a reduction of one coach in the sets working over the line. The stock sets rarely worked elsewhere and there had been no through coach workings from the Conwy Valley line for many years. *H.Rogers Jones.*

TAL Y CAFN & EGLWYSBACH

An historically interesting location, Tal y Cafn was known to the Romans during their occupation of this part of Wales, fording the river Conwy at this point. The Roman Camp was at Caerhun, on the opposite bank of the river. Close by is the estate of Lord Aberconway, at Bodnant near the village of Eglwysbach. It is now part of the National Trust and world famous for the ornamental garden and the staff with their horticultural skills.

Tal y Cafn was one of the original stations on the line, five miles from Llandudno Junction, and the first passing point on the branch. It was close to the river, and ferry boats competed for traffic until the First World War.

The main building is on the Down side, the Station Master's house being incorporated into the complex. The Booking Office adjoined the house. A General Waiting Room and Porters Room were detached from the main building and a small wooden hut served as a lamp room. The Up platform had a semi open shelter, similar to that at Llanrwst with the roof extended to afford some protection to passengers.

An LMS Standard Tappet Frame with $4\frac{1}{2}$" centres housing a set of 15 levers, of which nos. 4, 8 and 12 were spare, stood on a raised plinth at the south end of the Up platform and adjoining the hand operated level crossing. The frame was open to the elements although a cover was provided in the 1950's. Indicators and a long burning oil lamp were provided by the frame.

The single line token instruments were located in the Office.

There was limited provision for freight traffic, including facilities for handling livestock and horses. The Down line was extended beyond the level crossing and the connection with the single line formed a loop which gave access to a small platform on which stood a wooden goods store. Beyond was a Cattle Dock and pens. Access to the goods loop was by a small two lever ground frame whilst a second ground frame of two levers, which was locked by the train staff, controlled access to the single line. A short siding continued off the goods loop to terminate at buffer stops. A yard crane with lifting capacity of 5 tons stood adjacent to the track at this point.

With the rationalisation of services and withdrawal of facilities the Up loop line was taken out in 1965 and the shelter demolished, although the platform itself remained. The Goods Loop and siding were taken out whilst the fifteen lever frame was removed and replaced by a five lever frame on the former Down platform. Levers 1 and 2 controlled the Up Distant signal, levers 4 and 5 controlled the Down Distant whilst lever 3 controlled the level crossing gate lock.

Although staff were withdrawn from the station, the hand operated gates remain, normally positioned across the railway and an employee is stationed throughout the day to close them to road traffic.

107. Tal y Cafn. 1949. Immediately south of the station level crossing on the Down side was the Goods Loop which enabled livestock to be unloaded. The cattle pens were used but infrequently by this time. In the background beyond the point, and half hidden in the long grass, can be seen the yard crane, also little used. At the foot of the Up Home signal can be seen the two lever frame that controlled access to the Goods Loop, interlocked with the train staff. The signal however was controlled from the station frame on the Up platform, in this view towards Betws y Coed.   *Derek Chaplin.*

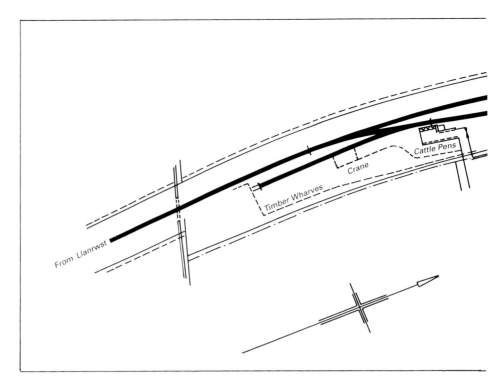

108. Tal y Cafn. 1949. The station looking towards Llandudno Junction. The level crossing gates were normally kept across the line. A small goods platform and shed were located on the passing loop Down line and not in the looped goods siding. Notice the small two lever ground frame controlled by the train staff which gave access to the Goods Loop. Once again we see the ubiquitous portable building, this time in use as a goods shed. If success was measured by the numbers of advertising signs, Astons must have had a substantial share of the market. *Derek Chaplin.*

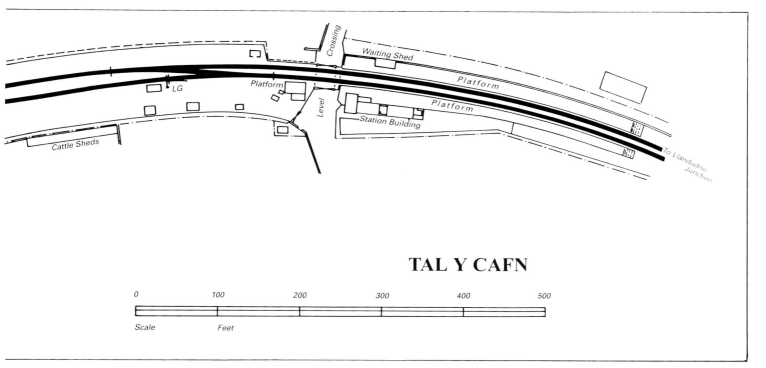

TAL Y CAFN

0	100	200	300	400	500

Scale   Feet

109. Tal y Cafn. 1949. An unidentifed Ivatt 2-6-2T Class 2 pulls over the level crossing with the daily Up freight from Blaenau Ffestiniog. The fireman leans out of the cab holding the train staff token which he will give to the porter signalman. Notice the LMS 'Hawkseye' station nameboard on the Down platform, just to the right of the small wooden building. *Derek Chaplin.*

110. Tal y Cafn & Eglwysbach. 1957. The low height of the platforms is brought home clearly in this view, showing the gap between the DMU body and the platform. The portable wooden steps were supposed to be kept in the shelter on each platform when not in use, but it seemed that passengers were somehow congregating on the wrong platform at busy times! The neat and tidy appearance of the station contrasts strongly with views taken in later days, when staff became disillusioned about job security, and in some cases not replaced when they retired or transferred elsewhere. Station Masters could sometimes be quite autocratic and the station staff were expected to keep the station tidy when not occupied with other tasks.   *J.W.T. House.*

111. Tal y Cafn & Eglwysbach. 1957. A four coach Derby Lightweight DMU sweeps around the curve into Tal y Cafn with a Blaenau Ffestiniog working. Many of the workings demanded four car sets to cater for the increase in passengers travelling, following the introduction of the units to the line, a phenomenon that was experienced by almost every other branch line service where the units replaced the steam workings. Drivers found them more satisfying to work than steam engines, mainly because they could keep clean throughout the day. Some regretted the isolation in the cab without a fireman, but no one admitted regretting the passing of steam.
J.W.T. House.

112. Tal y Cafn & Eglwysbach. 13th July 1966. An air of neglect hangs over the station, and although there has been no removal of track or buildings, the gardens have given way to weeds, the white platform edging has been allowed to wear away and the lamp posts stand minus the cases, so presumably the passengers have to struggle in the dark. However, the level crossing gates gleam in the distance, and the Up platform building looks in good order.   *C.L. Caddy.*

113. Tal y Cafn & Eglwysbach. March 1956. (Above). A gleaming new DMU stands at the Up platform with the 11.20am from Blaenau Ffestiniog. Contrast this picture with the lower picture on the previous page and compare how tidy the platforms looked when station staff were on hand to keep things in check. The popularity of the service is obvious as every seat seems occupied and indeed, inspection reveals that passengers were standing. Latterly during steam days it is doubtful whether this number of passengers would have travelled by train. *W.A. Camwell.*

114. Tal y Cafn & Eglwysbach. March 1956. Although the DMUs had taken over the regular passenger services on the line, some services were still worked by steam, and other views of this special working appear elsewhere in this book. Here, Stanier 2-6-2T No.**40133** of 6G coasts into Tal y Cafn station with the three coach empty stock train for the football supporters special Excursion from Blaenau Ffestiniog to Llandudno (Reporting Number W954A). Note the headlamp code. The fireman has built up his fire in readiness for departing the station, hence the smoke from the chimney.*W.A. Camwell.*

2nd · SINGLE		SINGLE · 2nd
5575	**GLAN CONWAY TO**	5575
	Glan Conway Tal-Y-Cafn & Eglwysbach	Glan Conway Tal-Y-Cain & Eglwysbach
	TAL·Y·CAFN & EGLWYSBACH	
	(M) 0/8 Fare 0/8 (M)	
	For conditions see over For conditions see over	

115. Tal y Cafn to Glan Conwy. 1954. (Lower). A hundred yards or so up the valley **40133** coasts past the Down distant signal for Tal y Cafn station. *H. Rogers Jones.*

116. Tal y Cafn to Glan Conwy. 1954. (Upper). The Class 3 2-6-2T locomotives ran the Conwy Valley line services from 1936 until they were replaced by the Ivatt Class 2 version, although they only completely replaced LNW design locomotives on the passenger services from 1946. The Stanier design engines were an improvement on the tender engines that worked previously, but were indifferent steamers and under powered, according to some crews. Here, **40130** hauls three non-corridor coaches on an afternoon working to Blaenau, skirting the estuary which was tidal. The line swings through ninety degrees as it follows the course of the river. Notice the boats moored on the mud flats alongside the line.

H. Rogers Jones.

117. Near Glan Conwy. 1954. (Centre). Ivatt 2-6-2T No.**41236** of 6G shed working bunker first back to Llandudno Junction with a lengthy Class K freight working from Blaenau Ffestiniog. Notice the mud flats in the river, for this was low tide. In rough weather, the water flooded the trackbed where the line curves at the extreme left hand edge of the picture, and gangers kept a vigilant eye on things, prepared to turn out in the middle of the night if the water encroached *H. Rogers Jones.*

118. Tal y Cafn to Glan Conwy. 1956. (Below). Another view of the track skirting the estuary, this time nearer Glan Conwy, showing a new DMU on an afternoon working to Blaenau Ffestiniog. Beyond the sweep of the curve can be seen a Permanent Way hut and past that the Down Distant signal for Tal y Cafn, half a mile away. The wide expanse of the river can be seen to advantage in this view. *H. Rogers Jones.*

GLAN CONWY

The village is located on the river estuary which is tidal for several miles up the valley, and the sandbanks that become exposed at low tides are frequented by gulls and wading birds who feed at low water. The village consisted of a few dwellings and the Church dedicated to St. Bridget. There are some historic remains near the village, including an old cromlech. The village increased in size in the 1960s, and much residential building took place in ribbon development along the road which runs parallel to the estuary and the railway line. Today, people commute to Llandudno, Colwyn Bay, for local empoyment, and with accelerated communications many people commute daily by rail to Chester. This was a factor that influenced the reopening of the station after initial closure in 1964.

Originally this station was called 'Llansantffraid' but was renamed Glan Conway in 1865. The station consisted of a single platform on the Down side, with the building housing the Station Master as well as the usual offices. The station itself was hemmed in by the river estuary, and at times flooding of the track occurred along this stretch of line, despite a protective retaining wall being build for some distance. There were no signals provided here. There was a trailing siding in the Down direction, which was controlled by the Train Staff, but little use was made of this until it became the site for a Camping Coach, and was a very popular venue.

The platforms, in common with all stations on the original Conway and Llanrwst Railway, were of low height, and steps were provided for passengers. There was some newspaper and limited parcels traffic, but receipts generally were poor, only boosted by the seasonal influx of tourists, and the station was closed in 1964. Public pressure caused it to be reopened as an unstaffed halt in 1970.

The stretch of line between Glan Conwy and Tal y Cafn is renown for its beauty, and in 1953, the Royal Train was worked up to a secluded spot by an ex LNW 0-8-0 G2A for the overnight stop, before being worked forward to Caernarfon by **42455** and **42157**, two of Bangor's Class 4 2-6-4T engines.

119. Glan Conwy. 1964. (Left). The station buildings and platform, taken from the back window of a Down DMU. The close proximity of the estuary can be seen, and the low wall afforded little protection to the track at high tide and in rough weather. Trains were repeatedly soaked at such times, and traincrews on steam working recount experiences when they were soaked to the skin at this point. No wonder the DMUs with their totally enclosed cab were appreciated. The platform is of low height, and steps were necessary to assist passengers alighting. *G.H. Platt.*

120. Glan Conwy. (Lower). For many years a Camping Coach was sited in the former goods siding on the Down side of the track from May to late September. It was a popular location, particularly in the summer months, and gave magnificent views of the estuary. The mud flats were more interesting to ornithologists rather than families with young children, but the Coach was generally booked up early throughout the season by families who used it as a centre and travelled to Llandudno and surrounding district. It is interesting to note the extensive use of concrete sleepering on sections of track that were affected by the river, although not necessarily at places where the two ran side by side. Occasionally, where the river burst its banks, the line up to a mile away could be affected. *W.G. Rear Collection.*

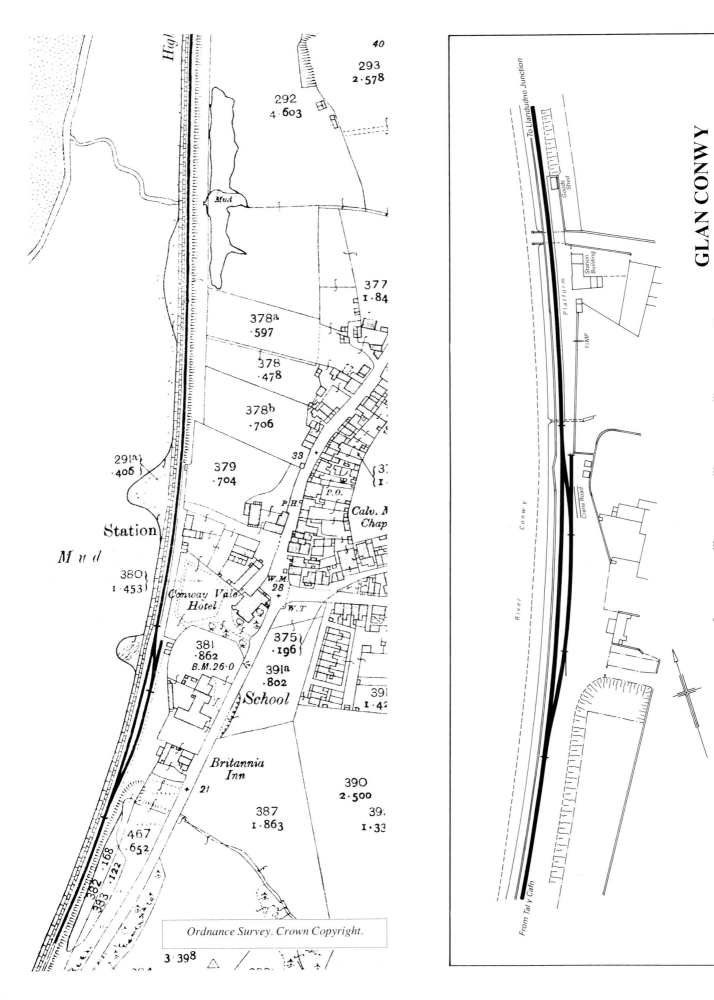

GLAN CONWY

To Llandudno Junction

Goods Shed

Station Building

Platform

1½ MP

River Conwy

Crane Road

From Tal y Cafn

400

300

200

100

0

Feet

Scale

40

293
2·578

292
4·603

Mud

377
1·84

378ᵃ
·597

378
·478

378ᵇ
·706

33

291ᵃ
·406

379
·704

P.O.

P H

Calv. M
Chap

Station

Mud

W.M
28

W.T

380
1·453

Conway Vale
Hotel

381
·862
B.M.26·0

375
·196

391ᵃ
·802

39
1·42

School

Britannia
Inn

21

390
2·500

39
1·33

387
1·863

467
·652

382 ·168

383 ·122

3·398

LLANDUDNO JUNCTION

Llandudno Junction station is located approximately halfway between Chester and Holyhead, 44 miles from the former. It was and still is the main intermediate point between the two towns and continues to play an important role in the working of traffic along the coast. As its title suggests, the station is a Junction on the main line between Chester and Holyhead, for the line to Llandudno and the branch to Blaenau Ffestiniog and Trawsfynydd.

The original (1848) station was located in the fork between the Llandudno and Holyhead lines. When the first section of the Conwy Valley line opened to Llanrwst in 1863, branch line trains ran into a separate platform on the south side of the Junction station. A refreshment room opened in 1864 and minor alterations and improvements were effected until the station was replaced, following quadrupling of the line from Colwyn Bay.

The present station was opened on 1st November 1897 and comprised six through lines with two bays at each end. The original station was west of the present one and when the latter was brought into use, the old station platforms and buildings were demolished. The construction of the new station meant that the original Conwy Valley line had to be diverted, the branch junction being relocated about half a mile east of the old. The original branch line formation was left intact, apart that is from its connection at the south end which was severed, and subsequently used for storing locomotives out of use. In 1984 the branch connection was moved east for a second time when a new freight terminal for oil, cement and general goods came into use. The locomotive department opened in 1879, the shed at this time being single ended and designed to house twelve locomotives. It was a sub-shed of Bangor. The depot was enlarged and altered to become an open-ended shed in 1899, holding twenty four engines with Blaenau Ffestiniog, Rhyl, Denbigh and Corwen as sub-sheds. A six road carriage shed was erected alongside the locomotive department at the same time. The Locomotive Department became independent of Bangor in April 1899 and was allocated the depot code 38. By 1923 the total engine allocation was 78. The structure was renovated and re-roofed in 1957. In LNWR and early LMS

121. Llandudno Junction. The approach to Llandudno Junction looking east, showing the tall LNWR signals for the Up Slow and Up Fast lines and the gantry for the Down Fast and Slow lines. *J.M. Dunn.*

122. Llandudno Junction. 10th July 1953. The Queen travelled overnight from Llanelli, arriving at Llandudno Junction at 3.25am. The Royal Train was then drawn beyond Glan Conwy by an unidentified G2A 0-8-0 locomotive. **42157** driven by H.O. Williams and fireman D.L. Jones, piloted **42455**, driven by G.L. Jones and fireman W.A. Griffiths, all from Bangor shed worked the Royal Special to Caernarfon, arriving there at 10.00am and seen here coming off the Conwy Valley branch. *W.G. Rear. Collection.*

days, the Motive power depot was considered less important than Bangor which had the pick of the long distance work. Under the reorganisation of the Motive Power structure plan entitled "*The Motive Power Area Locomotive Power Supply, Repair, Concentration and Garage Scheme*" inaugurated in 1933, Llandudno Junction became the concentration depot for the District, with Bangor, Holyhead and Rhyl becoming 'Garage Depots'. The shed coding 7A was introduced in 1935. Some work was transferred from Bangor at this time, although 7B retained the lodging turns to Euston with 'The Welshman' and some Bangor - Manchester Exchange - Liverpool Lime Street - Bangor workings. These were withdrawn at the commencement of the Second World War and were never reinstated, partly because Bangor men at that time were unwilling to learn the road beyond Crewe. The Euston work was transferred to Crewe North, and the Manchester or Liverpool Turns were taken over by Llandudno Junction or Chester. With the demise of steam and decline in loco hauled traffic, the Motive Power depot closed on 3rd October 1966 and the building demolished in the early 1980s. Traincrews now sign on at the Junction in the Offices which were located between the carriage shed and the freight sidings roads. The former Carriage Shed is used for stabling D.M.Units overnight.

Three signal boxes controlled the complex from early days, No.1 box housed a tumbler frame of 101 levers and located on the Down side between the occupation overbridge and the platforms.

This box also held the single line token apparatus for the Conwy Valley branch., No.2. box was located on the Up side, west of the platforms between the Dock road and the Warehouse siding, and housed an LNWR Tumbler 150 lever frame. It was replaced in 1985 by a new Power box built alongside the old box which was subsequently demolished. The Crossing box was originally located north of the level crossing behind the Junction Hotel, but was badly placed for sighting road traffic and was relocated in the early 1950s in the vee formed between the Llandudno [Town] tracks, and the Holyhead main line. With the completion of the flyover west of the station, Llandudno Junction Crossing box was closed and removed. The increasing traffic congestion previously caused by the level crossing gates then transferred to Conwy town.

Services diminished with the demise of steam, and the tracks serving the Down slow platform and bay platforms 2, 3 and 4 were removed. Nevertheless, three main platform faces remain in use, two on the Up side, and the Down Main line, No.1.bay line is now called platform 2. The Up side platforms are signalled for bi-directional working and trackwork through the station has been modified with surplus sidings taken out. The former Up goods line is now a Civil Engineering Maintenance Equipment siding, accessible from the Up and Down loop line which adjoins Platform 1. The connection is east of the platform.

123. Llandudno Junction. This elevated view shows the three arch overbridge (No.107) to the east of the station. The Conwy Valley line can just be seen through the left hand opening although of course by the time the line passed beneath this occupation bridge, it would be on the right hand side. From road level between the left and centre openings, a flight of steps gave access to the railway where a small hut stood adjacent to the Post Office pick up and receiving equipment. The running lines were, from left to right, Up slow (left hand arch), Up and Down fast (centre arch), Down slow and Branch (right hand arch). Note the double posted bracket signals to the right, the branch signal being in the "off" position.   *J.M. Dunn.*

124. Llandudno Junction. Taken from the same location as the previous picture but looking west, this view shows the Post Office apparatus and hut, the Down Slow line bracket signal and no.1. Signal Box in the middle distance, with the station beyond that. Notice also the extensive "guying" of signal posts, the wires required to cross the tracks to be not less than 20 feet above rail level. Generally, all signals above 25 feet in height were guyed. *J.M.Dunn.*

Local freight facilities were located on the Up side, access to the small yard being off the Up goods loop line at the west end of the station. A headshunt from the connection ran behind No.2. signal box, almost to the level crossing. Three sidings radiated from the headshunt, one with a warehouse located between one siding and the Up goods loop, another goods warehouse and a store off a parallel line with transfer to road loading facilities provided. The third line was used as a coal siding and there was also a siding for crippled wagons. Two sheds provided cover for road motor vehicles and a weighing machine and office were located at the road entrance to the yard. The goods shed on the Up side has been removed and the space taken over for industrial use. The waste land up the estuary and between the carriage shed and the eastern end of the complex has also been developed for industrial use with the developments resulting from the A.55 expressway and interchange roundabout now dominating the skyline.

Through freight and interchange sidings were provided on the down side, and comprised four sidings. Access to these by Up trains was across the carriage shed and motive power roads, but there was rarely any conflict. A siding to the small quay, which was originally used for transhipping river traffic, was also located on the Down side, but latterly was used to store coaching stock.

Both local and through freight traffic on the main line has changed over the years and a new freight terminal for oil, cement, and general goods was built in 1980 to deal with Freightliner traffic to and from Holyhead, stone traffic from Penmaenmawr, (mainly for Departmental use), a daily working from the Junction to Associated Octel Siding along the Amlwch branch, and the twice weekly Nuclear Fuel traffic to and from Trawsfynydd and Wylfa C.E.G.B. generating stations. Seven refuge sidings and Quay Siding stand between the Down platform and the Loco Sidings. Down freight trains requiring access to these sidings pass through the platform on the main line and set back into the yard. Passenger traffic has also undergone a radical change over the last twenty years, and apart from through Holyhead to Euston trains, the remainder of the services along the coast are in the hands of Multiple Unit stock of various configurations and vintage.

A detailed account of the station and its working was published in "*British Railways L.M.Region Magazine*" for August 1952. In that year, the station dealt with 73 through trains, 26 starting, and 22 terminating passenger services, daily. On summer Saturdays, up to 60 additional trains were dealt with. Approximately 100,000 passengers booked tickets from Llandudno Junction each year, with exchange passenger traffic amounting to many thousands more. There was a heavy transfer of passenger and parcels traffic at the station, particularly between Llandudno and Holyhead trains and Holyhead traffic on Llandudno trains. Trains were also made up and split here during their journeys.

Carriages were marshalled, cleaned and repaired in the large shed on the Down side, about 70 coaches daily being dealt with during summer months. The cleaning of the carriages was the responsibility of the Station Master.

The freight side dealt with approximately 2000 wagons weekly at the traffic yard, and local freight trains served stations to Menai Bridge, Llandudno and Blaenau Ffestiniog. Many main line freight trains also called here and in total, about twenty five separate freight trains were dealt with daily at the Junction. Parcels traffic was described in the account as 'moderate' and totalled more than 16,000 packages annually. Some traffic loaded at Colwyn Bay, Llysfaen and Abergele for destinations in the Up

direction were worked back to the Junction on Down line local trains to connect with through eastbound night trains to obviate frequent stopping of important freight trains. The through freight trains stopped at the Junction for locomotive and inspection purposes. Frequently, the traincrew also changed here. Some wagon repairs were effected in the yard.

At that time, the Crossing signal box was worked by two shifts, but was closed between 11.30pm and 4.40am. The gates were opened and closed about 70 times a day.

In 1952 the Station Master was Mr T.M. Dickenson. The staff comprised 16 clerical and 115 wages grades, The latter including 41 guards and 13 signalmen. The Senior Booking Clerk was Mr W.C. Hughes and Leading Parcels Porter was Mr Arthur E. Williams. Mentioned also were Signalmen H. Smith and G. Dickinson in No.2 box, and Dick Jones in the Crossing Box. Mr F. J. Burgess was the Goods Agent with Mr E.C. Elson his Chief Clerk and Mr J. Williams his Foreman. Carriage Shed Foreman was Mr David Jones, who also supervised the repair of crippled carriages on behalf of the Carriage & Wagon Engineer.' Stores Issuer in the Carriage Repairs Department was Mr J. McGrath, and Mr Ivor Jones was a Class 1 Carriage Repairer. Miss Dorothy Thompson operated the telephone switchboard and Miss Marian Evans was the telegraph clerk. Finally, the station's 'oldest' inhabitant was Porter Mr Edward Edwards, then 69, who had officially retired four years previously, but returned each summer to help out with the seasonal traffic. In addition, Llandudno Junction was an allotment station for platform staff for several local stations and supplied relief men as required.

125. Llandudno Junction. c.1938. A wealth of detail for the modeller! Note the Up Fast starter with the suspended bracket signals. An 0-6-0 "Cauliflower" with a Blaenau Ffestiniog train waits in No.3. bay. Three water tanks are visible and a van stands in the Engine Lie By siding alongside the enginemen's 'bothy'. The line across the foreground is the Up avoiding line.

126. Llandudno Junction. September 1938. (Upper). LNWR 0-6-2T No.27593 stands at the head of the 2.47pm [SO] to Betws y Coed in No.4 bay. The fireman stands propped against the platform name board with his driver, waiting for the guard's signal. Notice the wooden flooring of the platform extension and the gas lamp. The overhead wind bracing between the platform canopies was not provided when the station was new, being added some five years later, presumably after some telling experiences of the estuary weather at its roughest.

G.H. Platt.

127. Llandudno Junction. 11th May 1949. (Left). In almost the same location, eleven years later, Stanier 2-6-2T No.**40133** waits in No.4. bay at the head of the 10.53am Llandudno Junction to Blaenau Ffestiniog. After seventeen months of nationalisation, the side tanks still carry 'L.M.S.' although the number has been altered. Notice the workmen on the platform roof, catching up on a backlog of repairs held over from the war.

E.S. Russell.

128. Llandudno Junction. August 1956. (Lower). The DMUs had become established on the Conwy Valley line, and the 12.30pm from Blaenau Ffestiniog to Llandudno working pulls into No.4 platform. In the distance, a Class 'A' train for Chester passes under the road overbridge on the Up Fast line. *W.G. Rear.*

TRAFFIC

Llandudno Junction was the most important intermediate station between Chester and Holyhead, and most trains with the exception of the Up and Down 'Irish Mail' called here. Class 'A' workings along the coast were to and from Llandudno, Bangor or Holyhead to Crewe and Euston, Liverpool Lime Street or Manchester Exchange with portions for the alternative terminus detached and worked forward. Class 'B' or local traffic starting or terminating here worked to Blaenau Ffestiniog, Llandudno, Bangor, Caernarfon, Holyhead, Rhyl and Chester. Some Blaenau Ffestiniog trains commenced at Llandudno and worked through, whilst the best known named train, apart from "**The Irish Mail**" which worked through the Junction was 'The **Welsh Dragon**', a local push-pull operation between Rhyl and Llandudno which operated in the summer months only.

Up to 1967, during the winter period, traffic varied little during the week, with one or two extra late trains to various points on a Saturday. There was some excursion traffic throughout the year, partly to generate business for destinations such as Liverpool or Manchester. Sunday traffic was light throughout the year although there was some additional excursion traffic to the seaside resorts in May and September. From October to Easter, the Up and Down slow lines between Abergele and Llysfaen were taken out of day to day use but called upon to stable several hundred coaches. Coaching stock was also stored over the winter months on Deganwy Quay and Conway Morfa. These were removed in the week prior to the Bank Holiday and called into use on summer Saturdays as a last resort. In the summer months during the week there were daily excursions from the north west and midlands towns on most weekdays as well as local tourist traffic to cater for the weekly visitor. Handbills for the period included day trips to Ireland, the Land Cruise circular tours, combined rail and road excursions and daily trains to Llanberis, which also gave enough time for travellers to make a return trip to Snowdon Summit by the well known Snowdon Mountain Railway.

On summer Saturdays, traffic along the coast was almost at saturation level from early morning to late afternoon, a situation which necessitated switching in the small temporary intermediate block post at Mochdre & Pabo, a small signal box between Llandudno Junction No.1. and Colwyn Bay No.2., and

Conway Morfa, a location between Conway Station box and Penmaenmawr, to break up long sections and enable trains to be kept on the move. Manchester Locomotive Society conducted traffic surveys on peak Saturdays in 1953, 1954 and 1962. The 1954 exercise was the most comprehensive and provides an insight into the complexity of keeping traffic moving. Llandudno Junction platforms were occupied almost continuously with the Junction Crossing box causing additional chaos to the road traffic. The necessity to divide the regular Class 'A' trains here for forward working added to the problem, and 90 seconds to uncouple coach formations was considered reasonable. Through specials not booked to stop at the Junction were routed over the Avoiding Lines wherever possible. Prior to the war, when Bangor men worked through to Euston with the Up 'Welshman', two minutes was allowed to attach the stock from Llandudno and for the engine to take water, any delay over this allowance being booked against the enginemen by the Platform Inspector.

The R.S.D. notices for the period frequently indicated the need to stable up to sixty extra trains, of ten or eleven coaches, for several hours which could not all be accommodated at Llandudno, and were in some cases kept on the move until space became available to service the train. The situation was not unique to Llandudno Junction and both Bangor and Rhyl were hard pressed to store stock for a few hours. In Bangor's case, stock was moved to Menai Bridge and to Holyhead, whilst Rhyl stored stock on the Kinmel Park line off the Vale of Clwyd branch, and at Abergele. Extra staff were brought in to clean the stock although they frequently complained about the shortage of time to do a thorough job, due in part to the quick turn round. Some of the Saturday train movements were unbalanced, and the build up of stock was relieved by the following Monday's 'Horse and Carriage' workings that ran daily between Holyhead and Crewe and Ordsall Lane.

In the fifties and early sixties, there was considerable livestock traffic from Holyhead to Manchester and London, and it was not uncommon to find five or six cattle specials of fifty to sixty trucks each departing Holyhead in rapid succession. These workings were kept to weekdays wherever possible, but on one or two occasions, intruded into the Saturday traffic, which added to the congestion. The cattle were watered and fed at Holyhead prior

129. Llandudno Junction. 1956. Taken from the wooden extension to Platform 4 and bay 4 on the Down side, looking towards Colwyn Bay. Note the high elevation of No.1. box on the down side, whose frame had 101 levers. The water tank stood alongside No.3 bay in advance of the starter, at the foot of which was a ground disc signal for the Down shunting neck. The tall LNWR signals have been replaced by modern tubular upper quadrant arms, although the Down Slow bracket signals beyond the signal box still have a commanding height. Coaching stock is standing on the Down Avoiding Line, which was sometimes used to store stock for a brief period, rather than trip the coaches to the carriage sidings and back. *W.G. Rear.*

to loading onto the trains, and every effort was made to give the trains a clear run, even at the expense of the passenger traffic. Signalmen in the main boxes were kept fully occupied and it was normal practice to have an Inspector and a booking clerk in each box to keep traffic moving. Freight traffic on the line was kept to a minimum during the day. Movement of coaching stock to and from the carriage sidings caused blockages, as did locomotives moving on and off shed, and it was usual to stable locomotives and stock at Llandudno, where facilities were provided for turning and cleaning locomotives, with relief crews on duty to take over from traincrew to provide them with a rest period prior to working back to their home station.

130 Llandudno Junction. 1935. (Upper). 4-6-0 No. **5910** "*J.A. Bright*", a rebuilt Claughton of Bangor (21) Shed draws into the Up Fast platform with "The Welshman", from Pwllheli and Porthmadog to Euston. This was a Bangor No.1 Link lodging turn to Euston and the work was very tightly timed. The Claughton class of locomotives were subsequently replaced on this duty by 'Royal Scot' class engines, and attached to Camden for maintenance, rather than Bangor. Notice how high the coal is stacked. *G.H. Platt.*

131. Llandudno Junction. 5th July 1963. Britannia Class 4-6-2 No.**70027** "*Rising Star*" of Holyhead Shed (6J) stands at platform 2 with the 2.16pm Bangor to Llandudno working, Note the protective glass screen that sheltered passengers against the elements blowing off the estuary. *J.J. Davis.*

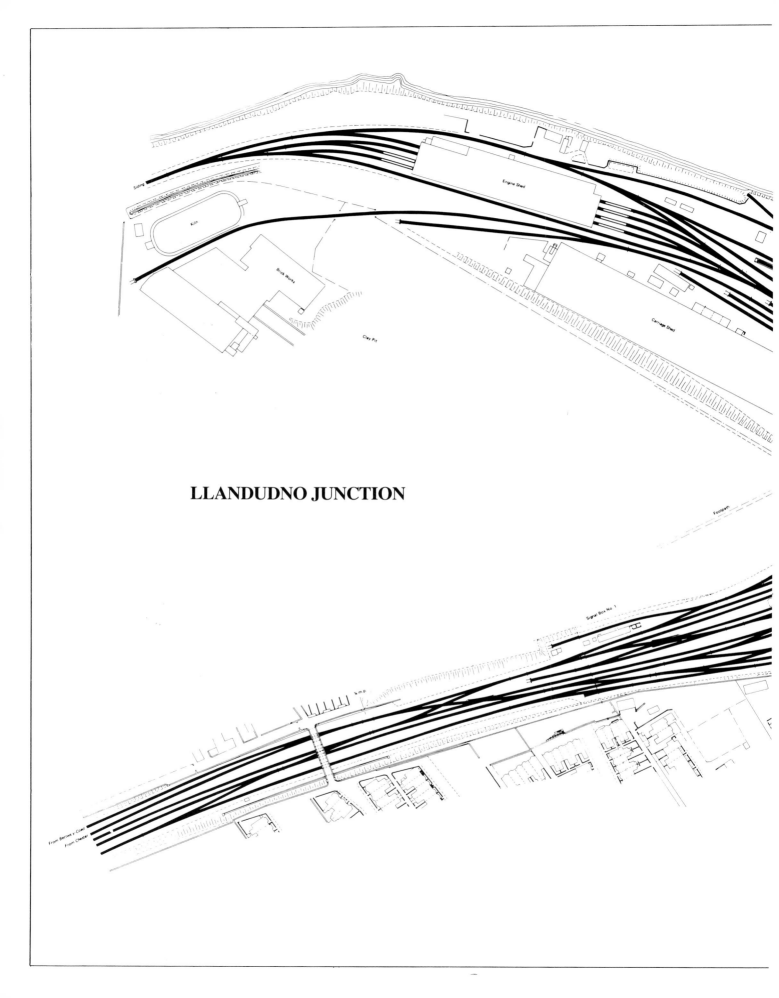

LLANDUDNO JUNCTION

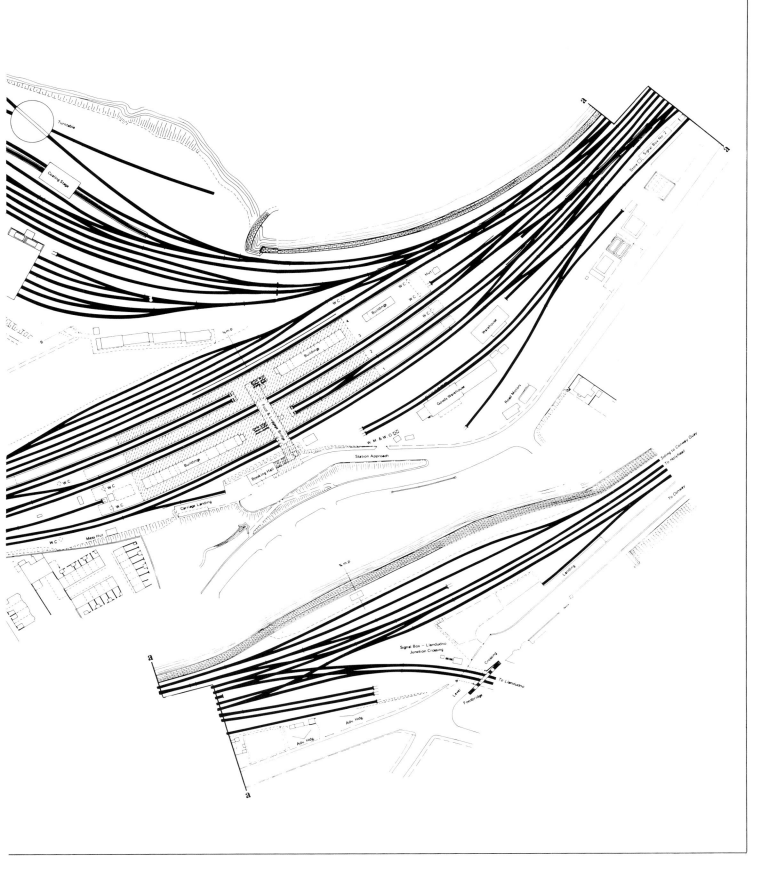

132. Llandudno Junction. (Right). The Carriage Shed, sidings and part of the Locomotive yard, seen from the west end of No.4. (Down Slow) platform. Between the platform line and the bracket signal is the Down Avoiding line. A fan of sidings extend parallel to the Down lines, and some through freight trains are marshalled here. There were six roads in the carriage shed, and running stocks of loco coal was stored in two sidings alongside the shed. Just visible on the right hand edge of the picture is the water tank which supplied all the columns on the site.

J.M. Dunn.

133. Llandudno Junction. 1938. (Centre). Another view of the Carriage Shed, with LNW 0-6-2T No.**7841** standing on No.4. road. Behind the loco can be seen the large water tank over the Coaling Stage. Mineral wagons with running coal stocks for the loco department fill the sidings and a private owner wagon for Bersham Colliery can just be seen over the low shed in the foreground. The loco crew are enjoying a break, sitting on sleepers close to their loco. In the foreground can be seen the tracks of the sorting sidings.

G.H. Platt.

134. Llandudno Junction. September 1948. (Lower). LNW 5' 6" 2-4-2T No.**6710** stands in the loco yard whilst shed staff prepare the engine. A cleaner is standing on the front buffer beam attending to the smokebox. A Fairburn 2-6-4T from Bangor shed is partially concealed by the older engine. The shed roof is in poor order with many panes of glass missing. It will be a few years before the roof is replaced.

G.H. Platt.

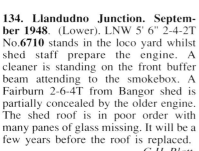

135. Llandudno Junction. (Above). The shed in early L.M.S. days, with the roof in better order than seen in the previous photograph. The interior was, by all accounts, a dismal place for the Mechanical Staff to work, and proximity of the estuary meant that in the winter months it was a dank and depressing place. Notice the roof ventilators, which were supposed to dissipate the smoke, but seldom did!. The structure changed little until the building was renovated and re-roofed in the late 1950s. *L.& G.R.P. No.2268.*

136. Llandudno Junction. 28th January 1934. (Centre). The first Conwy Valley line was superceded in 1897 when the course of the line was moved eastward, when the new station was opened. The old line was retained and passed to the Locomotive Department, although it was severed at its southern end. The LMS regularly used this line to store locomotives out of service over the winter months. Seen here are **5371, 5406, 7674, 7596, 5402, 5407, 5354, 5341, 5409, 5405, 5343, 5372, 5373, 5404, 6783, 8755, 8861** and **8385.** in a clean and well maintained state. *W.A. Camwell.*

137. Llandudno Junction. 1962. (Lower). Llandudno Junction was responsible for snow clearance on the North Wales lines and kept a plough on hand for the winter season which could be attached to the front of a range of locomotives, usually Fowler 0-6-0. It came as a surprise when a GWR 0-6-0 was designated to this duty and attached to the shed. It will be remembered that the winter of 1962/3 was a particularly nasty one, and the loco was seen at work on several occasions. **3208** is seen here beyond the turntable road out of steam, and a row of tank engines can also be seen behind the tender. *E.N. Kneale.*

MOTIVE POWER

October 1926
5009, 5052, 5117, 5140, 5146, 5155, 5159, 5167, 5177
5216, 5245, 5310, 5368, 5405, 5457, 5472, 5500, 5511
5540, 5705, 5715, 5722, 5732, 5736
6528, 6537, 6539, 6579, 6597, 6617, 6622, 6633, 6639,
6640, 6668, 6678, 6684, 6694, 6716, 6750
7552, 7553, 7583, 7599, 7600, 7607, 7628, 7656, 7730,
7734, 7779, 7804, 7805
8059, 8332, 8341, 8342, 8364, 8389, 8393, 8397, 8450,
8472, 8502, 8508, 8552, 8574, 8587, 8608
8909, 9123, 9617, 9618, 9619, 9637

December 1937
79, 82, 105, 107, 495, 5035, 5045, 5048, 5052, 5070,
5130, 5219, 5235, 5236, 5246, 5253, 5371, 5444
6635, 6667, 6676, 6679, 6682, 6713, 6748,
8337, 8385, 8401, 8503, 8521, 8616
25279, 25297, 25348, 25371, 25373, 25392,
27571, 27593, 27597, 27604, 7803

January 1948
83, 87, 123, 133, 137, 524, 671, 675, 925, 936,
1086, 1093, 1118, 1119, 1150, 1151, 1156, 1161
2954, 2971, 3877, 4389,
4860, 4911, 5112, 5253, 5301, 5303, 5346, 5370
6747, 7796, 28337, 28505, 28521

ENGINE WORKINGS

Little recorded information is available about train work-ing on the Conwy Valley line before 1936. It is understood that prior to the line reaching Betws y Coed, Llanrwst engine shed had three sets of men who worked alongside Llandudno Junction men. When the line was extended to Betws y Coed, a small shed was built there, but there is no evidence that it was brought into service or had men attached. When the extension to Blaenau Ffestiniog was opened, a combined carriage and locomotive shed was constructed there. Llanrwst shed was closed in 1881.

Blaenau Ffestiniog shed in L.N.W.R. days had seven sets of men and two locomotives, with the Junction providing the locomotives which stabled overnight. Work attached to the shed diminished during early L.M.S. days and it is understood that by the close, this had been reduced to three sets of men and one loco stabled overnight. When the shed closed on 14th September 1931 the men transferred to Llandudno Junction.

Before 1936, the motive power for the branch consisted of 2-4-2T and 0-6-2T tank engines and were usually to be found on the short trips to Betws y Coed, with some duties worked as Push-Pull or 'Motor' trains. 18" goods 0-6-0 tender engines worked most of the passenger and all freight services over the whole length of the line. The tender engines were turned at Blaenau Ffestiniog, and during winter months great difficulty was experienced in keeping the turntable pit clear of snow, requiring all hands available to assist in the push.

About 1936, Fowler design Class 3 2-6-2T locomotives were introduced to the line, replacing the 0-6-0 on the passenger duties, which eliminated the need to turn at Blaenau. These were a distinct improvement on their predecessors, in comfort if not in steaming capabilites, and by 1937, there were four engines of this wheel arrangement covering the passenger work. The Fowler

138. Llandudno Junction. 1963. The Motive Power depot after rebuilding in 1957 was a much improved place to work, according to the Mechanical staff. Seen on shed are **84009, 78058, 44913**, and unidentified Class 5 on No.2. road outside the shed and the tender of another in front of it, and **84003**.

E.N. Kneale.

engines were preferred to the more modern taper boiler Stanier designed versions, which were indifferent steamers. The LNWR 18" 0-6-0 goods still worked the freight turns which persisted until the 1950s. Although engines of up to power classification 5 were permitted, the powers that be seemed reluctant to exceed Power Class 3 until the end of steam, when finally Class 5 4-6-0 tender engines worked the daily goods. More Stanier locomotives replaced the parallel boiler version which had a monopoly of the line until the early 1950s when Ivatt 2-6-2T Class 2 Nos. **41236-9** took over the workings, much to the relief of the traincrews, and remained on the line until they were replaced by Derby Lightweight D.M.U.s in 1956. Ivatt 2-6-2Ts continued to work the daily freight until they were replaced by Class 5 4-6-0s.

Full details about Llandudno Junction Engine Workings for June 1951 are available. There were 22 booked duties on Mondays and Thursdays, twenty on Tuesdays, Wednesdays and Thursdays, with twenty five on a Saturday and five on a Sunday allocated to seven Class 5 4-6-0s, six 4-4-0 Compounds, five Class 3 2-6-2T, two 18" Class 2F 0-6-0 and a Class 2P 4-4-0, whilst the Goods engine workings were covered by one LMS Class 3F STD 0-6-0T, two Class 4F 0-6-0 and a Class 1P 2-4-2T.

ENGINEMEN'S WORKINGS

Llandudno Junction shed in common with other depots operated a Link structure with the Senior drivers working the prestige long distance turns whilst the younger drivers worked their way through the links from the preparation and disposal links, to the goods link, which was when they worked over the branch. Firemen started off in the Turning and Goods link before moving to the Passenger duties, and then worked back through the links as they achieved seniority. By the time they had passed out, they would be working in the Goods or Turning links whilst awaiting promotion, and getting the occasional driving turn. Once registered, it was a question of waiting for an opportunity to advance through the links, which took many years, promotion being slow.

No details are available about the pre-war Enginemen's Workings other than accounts from former drivers. It would appear that branch workings were normally kept to the lower passenger links. Senior drivers would work a turn over the branch on a Rest Day to maintain route knowledge. Drivers had a much wider route card, which included Saturday Only jobs to Birkenhead, Birmingham and Coventry, and to Leamington Spa as well as Crewe, Liverpool Lime Street and Manchester., No.3. Link men worked regularly to Llanberis and had a motor train duty from the Junction to Caernarfon, then to Bethesda, returning to Bangor and back to the Junction. In 1939, drivers were taken over the Afonwen line, route learning to Pwllheli in anticipation of working through trains to Butlin's Camp, which was under construction. The late Bill Griffiths remembered firing over the line a couple of times, but with the camp being taken over by the Royal Navy for the duration, the facility was dropped and apart from a brief resurrection during 1956 during D.M.U. familiarisation trials already mentioned, Junction men never worked regularly over the Afonwen branch again.

By 1951, the Top Link consisted of four turns, working to Manchester, Liverpool, Crewe and Holyhead., No.2. Link consisted of eight sets of men, working mostly passenger and some freight turns along the coast., No.3. Link consisted of twelve sets of men, which included the passenger work along the branch

whilst the Goods Link consisted of another twelve sets of men who worked over most routes. A Turning link of three sets of men and one Control Set completed the regular booked work.

Twelve turns covered all weekday work on the branch with thirteen turns on a Saturday. Most work was a single trip from Llandudno Junction to Blaenau and back, and two turns worked to Betws y Coed and return on weekdays. The freight trips were somewhat lengthy duties, and if crews had worked out and home the duty would have exceeded the Drivers working hours so traincrews changed footplates at Blaenau, working out on a passenger trip and returning with a freight. In one case, traincrews changed footplates twice, working passenger to Blaenau, Freight back to Llanrwst and then passenger to Llandudno Junction.

The Link structure had changed by 1960. Diesel Multiple Units had taken over all the passenger workings on the branch as well as some workings on the main line. The drivers in the senior No.1. link had opted to take life at a slower pace and their work on steam included a couple of trips to Llandudno and back and a trip up the Conwy valley on the freight. It was regarded by some as the 'Old Man's Link'. No.2., link also consisted of four sets, and worked to Manchester, Liverpool Lime Street and Crewe., No.3. Link comprised six sets and worked mainly along the coast., No.4 Link comprised eight sets, and according to information, which has not been verified, worked D.M.U.s on the branch and between the Junction, Rhyl and Bangor., No.5. Link was the residue of the passenger and freight work and comprised ten sets, whilst No.6. Link was the Turning link and comprised three sets of men.

DRIVERS.

The only list of drivers available dates from 1960 and is included here, together with their pay number. The list was compiled from the Ashpit Register, and if anyone has been omitted, I regret this and apologise.

1....R.T.Jones	2....W.H.Parry	3....E.Davies
4....Tom Gill	5....W.Evans	6....J.W.Jones
7....A.L.Jones	8....W.O Griffiths	9....F.D.Williams
10....R.J.Owen	11....J.G.Thomas	12....W.H.Parry
13....J.G.Jones	15....C.Pritchard	16....T.R.Davies
17....H.Parry	18....M.Roberts	19....G.H.Edwards
20....H.I.Jones	21....G.Blanch	22....C.Lynch
23....J.W.Gough	24....W.G.Jones	25....G.C.Jones
26....L.P.Jones	27....P.Bethell	28....W.L.Williams
29....E.E.Parry	30....J.H.Edgerton	31....C.Roberts
32....D.Roberts	33....T.R.Jones	37....H.Jenkins
38....J.L.Roberts	39....J.V.Williams	40....E.W.Thomas
41....W.Lloyd	42....E.Jones	43....E.H.Williams
44....T.W.Hughes	45....H.W.Hughes	46....E.Williams
47....G.Williams	48....C.O.Williams	49....I.D.Garland
50....W.A.Roberts	51....J.Davies	52....F.O.Raw
53....W.J.Williams	54....G.Griffiths	55....K.Jones [1]
56....E.W.Hughes	57....W.C.B.Williams	64....H.Shields
66....A.Roberts	67....K.Jones	68....E.Hughes
70....J.L.Williams	71....R.D.Parker	72....W.R.Jennings
73....H.E.Roberts	74....W.Price	77....W.D.Morris
78....J.R.Dines	79....T.A.Hughes	80....D.M.Jones
81....D.J.Evans	83....J.T.Roberts	84....J.N.Williams
86....K.E.Davies	87....T.W.Smart	88....G.McKean
89....L.M.Evans	90....B.A.Edwards	92....R.I.Williams
93....R.E.Roberts	94....R.Welsh	95....K.Jones [2]
96....W.R.Hughes	97....A.L.Griffiths	99....N.Jones.

139. Llandudno Junction. 1964.
(Upper). The Down Slow platform was an exposed place for most of the year, and the LNWR were sensitive to the comforts of their passengers. They erected this protective screen that ran the length of the building, which afforded some protection. The new Motive Power Depot offices can just be seen behind the water tank pillar.

D. Thompson.

140. Llandudno Junction. 1938. The North Wales Coast was the last haunt of many of the former LNWR passenger locomotives, which worked out their final days on local services. Here Precursor Class 4-4-0 No.**25277** "*Oberon*" stands on the Down Fast line whilst working as light engine through the platform road to gain access to the shed, and is held by the starter. An Inspector, complete with bowler hat hides behind the water tank! The 150 lever No.2. signal box is visible, in front of Fyffes Banana Store. On the Up side beyond the Up Goods Loop is one of the Warehouses in the small yard, and behind that can just be seen a carriage body mounted on blocks, which served as an Office and second store.   *G.H. Platt.*

141. Llandudno Junction. 1938.
(Below). Small boiler un-named Claughton No.**5994,** still sporting a smoke box number plate, draws into the Up Fast platform with a Llandudno to Manchester Exchange working. A variety of goods wagons stand in the Up Goods Loop line.   *G.H. Platt.*

142. Llandudno Junction. 14th September 1949. (Above). The trackwork at the west end of the station was complex, as this view shows, with the main line to Holyhead sweeping round to the left whilst the Llandudno branch forks right. Note No.2 signal box. The Crossing box has not been relocated and can just be seen under the footbridge and alongside the Hotel. The junction to the left of the picture served the engine shed whilst the scissors crossover enabled trains from both the avoiding and slow lines to gain the Holyhead line without conflicting with movements to the Llandudno branch.

Britsh Railways London Midland Region.

143. Llandudno Junction. 8th August 1956. (Below). The Crossing Box was relocated to give better visibility to the road traffic. The wagons in the foreground are on the Quay line which ends on a jetty alongside the river. Lines to and from Llandudno sweep off to the right. It is difficult to envisage that this convergence of rails was the site for the first Llandudno Junction station. Only the Junction Hotel, re-named Maelgwyn, survives to give any idea of location.

British Railways London Midland Region.

144. Llandudno Junction. 14th September 1949. (Above). Taken from the signal gantry in front of No.2 signal box and looking east, this view shows the small goods yard on the Up side, and the sweep of the platforms. A variety of motive power and stock is on display. From left to right, the lines were identified as follows:- Up avoiding, Up Slow (Platform 1.), which came in from the Llandudno branch. The third and fourth lines ended in the Up bay platforms 1 and 2. Immediately to the right of the walking boards, are the fast lines. *British Railways London Midland Region.*

145. Llandudno Junction. 14th September 1949. (Below). This view gives a slightly different perspective of the station complex, from the site of where the replacement Junction Crossing box will be located. Note the miniature arm shunting signals in the foreground. The age of mechanical track maintenance has not yet fully arrived and it is noticeable that ballast edges are tidy and surplus/spare materials are neatly stacked away from the running lines. *British Railways London Midland Region.*

146. Llandudno Junction. 14th September 1949. (Above). Taken from the Up bracket signal on the Holyhead line, looking toward the station. To the left is the Up refuge siding in which slow moving goods trains were sometimes reversed. The space occupied by smallholding is the site of the former Llandudno Junction station. The wagons to the right are on the quay siding, at a point near to where the Down side buildings of the old Junction station were located. The Conwy Valley branch followed the shore line, a ticket platform once being situated at a point near the locomotive in the middle distance. *British Railways London Midland Region.*

147. Llandudno Junction. 14th September 1949. (Below).Taken from the footbridge over the Llandudno line, and showing the level crossing gates. It would be interesting to know if these gates and posts are the same as those in plate 149 (see over). Above the wagons to the left, note the replacement bracket signal in situ ready to replace the 4 doll LNWR structure. Most of the old signalling has been dispensed with although the east end was to retain examples for the next couple of decades. Note the carriage shed across the estuary and the space occupied, indicating the extensive facilities available. The water tank was located over the locomotive coaling stage. *British Railways London Midland Region.*

148. Llandudno Junction. 1938.
(Upper). Two light engines heading
for Llandudno approach the level
crossing after coming off shed. The
crossing and gates were a continual
headache for the signalman on duty
at the crossing box, behind the
camera, who had to open and close
the gates up to seventy times on a
busy summer Saturday. His job was
not made any easier by the poor
sighting along Conway Road, which
was obscured by the Hotel.

G.H. Platt.

149. Llandudno Junction. 1896.
The first Llandudno Junction station was located further west and the
Llandudno line platforms came up
to the level crossing gates. On the
opposite side of the road are fields
where later the Crosville depot
would be built. Notice also the signal
box behind the row of wagons in the
centre of the picture, and the three
arm bracket signal in front of it.
Notice also the signal arm suspended from the footbridge and the
unusual location of the starting signal to the right behind the wall. On
the far platform, a notice board -
made up of station nameboard
components - advertises the North
Western Hotel at Blaenau Ffestiniog whilst in the foreground a boy
porter does a balancing act on the
handles of a platform trolley.

British Railways L.M.R.

BETTWS-Y-COED & FESTINIOG BRANCH.—(SINGLE LINE.)

TRAIN STAFF STATIONS.—Llandudno Junction, Tal-y-Cafn & Eglwysbach, Llanrwst, Bettws-y-Coed, Dolwyddelen, and Blaenau Festiniog.

Passenger Trains can cross each other only at Tal-y-Cafn, Llanrwst, Bettws-y-Coed, and Dolwyddelen.

STATIONS. Down Trains. WEEK DAYS.		1 Mixed and Mail See Note. a.m.	2 Goods CS a.m.	3 Goods Thurs only. a.m.	4 Empt. Coach a.m.	5 Goods Thurs excep. 2 a.m.	6 Pas a.m.	7 Pas a.m.	8 Pas a.m.	9 Seas'n Exc'n a.m.	10 Pas a.m.	11 Light Engin Goods CS S a.m.	12 3 p.m.	13 Pas p.m.	14 Pas p.m.	15 Pas p.m.	16 Pas See Note. p.m.	17 Pas p.m.	18 Mixed See Note. p.m.	19 Pas Thurs only. p.m.	20 Pas and Mails. Sun. a.m.
Llandudno Junction	dep	4 25	5 0	6 15	6 45		8 20	8 50	10 10	10§22	11 30		12 40	2 0	2 30	3 40	5 30	6 55	8 5	10 45	5 10
Glan Conway	,,			6 23		7 8	8 24		10 14		11 34		X	2 4		3 44	5 34	6 59	8 9	10 49	
Tal-y-Cafn & Eglwysbach {arr		4 39	5§20	6 38	6 53	7 23	8 22	8 58	10 22	10 40	11 42		1 10	2 12		3 52	5 42	7 7	8 15	10 57	5 21
{dep		4 40	5§50	6 45	6§53	8 0	8 36	9 4	10 23	10§43	11 43		1 30	2 13	2§38	3 54	5 43	7 9	8 21	10 59	5 23
Abbey Siding	,,																				
Tan Lan Siding	,,																				
Llanrwst and Trefriw {arr		4 55	6 §5	7 2	7 1	8 20	8 47	9 14	10 33		11 52		1 45	2 23	2 46	4 4	5 53	7 19	8 36	11 9	5 33
{dep		5 10	6 §5	7 30	7 §5	10 0	8 52	9 16	10 35	10§51	11 55		2 15	2 26	2 48	4 6	5 55	7 21	8 45	11 11	5 35
BETTWS-Y-COED {arr		5 20	6§15	7 45	7 12	10 15	8 59	9 23	10 42	10 58	12 2		2 30	2 33	2 55	4†13	6 2	7 29	8 55	11 18	5 42
{dep		5 25	6§15	8 0		11 18	9 3		10 47		12 7	1 45	3 15	2 37			6 6		8 58		5 47
Pontypant	,,	5 40					9 15		10 59		12 19						6 18		9 10		
DOLWYDDELEN {arr		5 46	6 35	8 20		11 40	9 19		11 3		12 23	2 §1	3 41	2 53			6 22		9 14		6 2
{dep		5 52	7 0	8 45		11 45	9 22		11 6		12 33	2§30	4 5	2 56			6 25		9 16		6 4
Roman Bridge	,,	5 59				X	9 29		11 13		12 40		X	3 3			6 32		9 23		
Greaves Sdng & Oakley Siding	,,																				
BLAENAU FESTINIOG	,,	6 12	7 20	9 6		12 5	9 41		11 25		12 52	2 50	4 30	3 15			6 44		9 35		6 20

STATIONS. Up Trains.		21 Pas a.m.	22 Pas Mondays only during August only. a.m.	23 Pas a.m.	24 Pas a.m.	25 Pas p.m.	26 Pas noon	27 Goods CS S O p.m.	28 Pas S O p.m.	29 Pas p.m.	30 Goods and Empt. Carrs. p.m.	31 Seas'n Exc'n p.m.	32 Goods 2 p.m.	33 Pas p.m.	34 Pas p.m.	35 Mixed Work men's Coach S 3 p.m.	36 Empt. Coach p.m.	37 Pas 3 p.m.	38 Empt. Carrs. and Goods p.m.	39 Goods CS p.m.	40 Empt. Carrs. p.m.	41 Sunday. Pas p.m.
BLAENAU FESTINIOG	dep	6 35		8 5	9 45		12 15	12 55	12 55	2 0			3 30		5 30	5 50		7 55		7 5		6 20
Greaves Sg & Oakley Sg	,,																					
Roman Bridge	,,	6 47		8 17	9 57		12 27		1 7	2 12			X		5 42	6 3		8 7	S			
DOLWYDDELEN {arr		6 52		8 22	10 2		12 32		1 12	2 17			3 55		5 47	6 9		8 12		7 30		6 36
{dep		6 54		8 24	10 4		12 35	1§17	1 14	2 19			4 15		5 49	6 15		8 14		7 35		6 38
Pontypant	,,	6 58		8 28	10 8		12 39		1 18	2 23			X		5 53	6 20		8 18				
BETTWS-Y-COED {arr		7 10		8 40	10 20		12 51	1 35	1 30	2 35			4 35		6 5	6 33		8 30		8 0		6 53
{dep		7 15	7 35	8 43	10 25	12 5	12 56		1 35	2 40		5 0	5 30	5 19	6 15	6 34	7 40	8 35		9 5		11 25	6 58
Llanrwst and Trefriw {arr		7 22	7 42	8 50	10 32	12 12	1 3		1 42	2 47			5 45	5 26	6 22	6 41	7 50	8 42		9 19			7 5
{dep		7 26	7 44	8 54	10 34	12 14	1 5			2 50	3 25	5 §6	6 40	5 28	6 25		8 0	8 44	9 0	9 25		11§32	7 7
Tan Lan Siding	,,									† See Note												
Abbey Siding	,,																					
Tal-y-Cafn & Eglwysbach {arr		7 36	7 52	9 3	10 42	12 24	1 15			3 0	3 40		6 55	5 38	6 35		8 15	8 54	9 15	9§45		7 17
{dep		7 37	7§52	9 6	10 43	12 25	1 17			3 2	4 0	5§14	7 20	5 43	6 37		8 30	8 56	9 25	9§45		11§42	7 19
Glan Conway {arr		7 45		9 13	10 49	12 32	1 24			3 9	4 15			5 50	6 45			9 4				7 27
{dep		7 46		9 16	10 50	12 33	1 26			3 11	4 20		X	5 52	6 47			9 7	X			7 29
Llandudno Junc.	arr	7 49	8 +2	9 19	10 53	12 36	1†29			3 14	4 25	5§22	7 40	5 55	6 50		8 45	9 10	9 45	10 5		11 55	7 33

No. 1 is a Mixed Train between Llandudno Junc. and Bettws-y-Coed only. Engine working No. 5 comes out of the Shed at 6.0 a.m. to form the Train.

No. 14—The empt. coaches to be returned to Llandudno J. on No. 50 leaving Bettws-y-Coed at 5.15 p.m. for Llanrwst.

No. 18 — Mixed Train between Llandudno Jct. and Bettws-y-Coed only. When not conveying Goods Vehicles the time allowed between Tal-y-Cafn and Llanrwst will be 10 mins. & between Llanrwst & Bettws-y-Coed 7 mins.

No. 24—Bettws-y-Coed to wire Llandudno Jct. if there are any passengers in this train for the 10.50 a.m. from Llandudno.

Public Bills arrival at Llandudno Junct. 10.55

No. 26—Public Bills arr. Llandudno Jct. 1.32 p.m.

No. 32—Stops at Tal-y-Cafn and Glan Conway only for Tranships for Liverpool & Manchester, and Cattle Traffic.

The Tranship Vans on No. 32 to be marshalled as follows:—

Engine, Park Lane Van, Liverpool Rd. Van, Crewe Chester & Conway Vans.

The last three to be put off in the Warehouse at Llanrwst, and be taken forward by No. 58.

Blaenau Festiniog Tickets of all Down Trains to be collected at Roman B. except No. 20, which must be collected at **Dolwyddelen**.

The arrival times at Roman Bridge of Nos. 1, 6, 8, 10, 12, 16, & 18, are two minutes earlier than the times shewn, two minutes being allowed at Roman Bridge for collection.

150. Betws y Coed. 27th May 1947. LMS 0-6-2T No. **7841** of Llandudno Junction shed (7A), pulls into Betws y Coed with the 2/00pm from the Llandudno, comprising two non-corridor coaches. After a wait of 80 minutes, it formed the 4/09pm back to Llandudno Junction. *W.A. Camwell.*

L.M.S. Passenger Working Time Table. July 2nd to September 24th 1939.

BLAENAU FESTINIOG AND LLANDUDNO JUNCTION.

WEEKDAYS.

Stations (with mileages):

Miles.	Station
	BLAENAU FESTINIOG — dep.
4¾	Roman Bridge — arr./dep.
6¼	Dolwyddelen — arr./dep.
7¾	Pontypant — arr./dep.
12¼	Bettws-y-Coed — arr./dep.
16	Llanrwst & Trefriw — arr./dep.
19	Dolgarrog — arr.
22	Tal-y-Cafn & Eglwysbach — arr./dep.
25¼	Glan Conway —
27¼ (276)	LLANDUDNO JN. — arr.

Column numbers (WEEKDAYS): 1, 2, 4, 5, 6, 7, 8, 10, 11, 12, 13, 14, 15, 16, 17, 18, 19, 20, 22, 23, 24, 25, 26, 27, 31, 32, 33

WEEKDAYS—continued columns: 34, 35, 36, 37, 38, 39, 40, 42, 43, 44, 45, 46, 47, 48, 49, 50, 51, 52, 53, 54

SUNDAYS.

Columns: 56, 58, 59, 60, 61, 62, 63, 64, 65, 66, 67

LLANDUDNO JUNCTION AND BLAENAU FESTINIOG.

WEEKDAYS

Stations (with mileages):

Miles.	Station
	LLANDUDNO JUNCTION — dep.
1½	Glan Conway —
5¼	Tal-y-Cafn & Eglwysbach — arr./dep.
8¼	Dolgarrog —
11¼	Llanrwst & Trefriw — arr./dep.
15	Bettws-y-Coed — arr./dep.
19½	Pontypant —
21	Dolwyddelen — arr./dep.
22½	Roman Bridge — arr./dep.
27¼	BLAENAU FEST'G — arr.

Column numbers (WEEKDAYS): 1, 2, 3, 4, 5, 6, 7, 8, 9, 10, 11, 12, 13, 14, 15, 17, 18, 19, 20, 21, 22, 23, 25, 26, 27, 28, 29, 31, 32, 33

WEEKDAYS—continued columns: 34, 35, 36, 37, 38, 39, 40, 41, 42, 43, 44, 45, 46, 47, 48, 49, 50, 51, 52, 53

SUNDAYS.

Columns: 55, 56, 57, 58, 59, 60, 61, 62, 63, 64, 65, 66

L.M.S. Freight Working Time Table. May 1st to September 24th 1939.

WEEKDAYS.

Miles	For continuation of trains from junctions, see page			1	2	4	5	6	8	9	10	12	13	14
				Freight.	Freight.	Freight.		Freight. SUSPENDED commencing July 8.	Freight SUSPENDED commencing July 3.	Freight. Commences July 3.	Freight.	Freight. SUSPENDED commencing July 3.	Freight.	Freight to Llandudno.
								See note	See note					
				Q	SX	SO		SO	SX	SX	SO	SX	SO	Q SX
				a.m.	a.m.	a.m.		p.m.	a.m.	p.m.	p.m.	p.m.	p.m.	p.m.
0		BLAENAU FESTINIOG ⊕	dep.	8 25	..	....	....	....	10 25	1 10	2 5	2 25	2 25	....
		Greaves' & Oakley's Sidings ..		8 30	Commences July 3.	Commences July 8.	..	..	..	..	..	..	..	SUSPENDED commencing July 3.
4¾		Roman Bridge		....			....	....	X	....	....	....	....	
6½		Dolwyddelen .. .. ⊕	arr.	..			..	..	10 40	1 25	..	..	2*40	
			dep.	....			....	....	11 45	1 40	2*20	2*40	2*45	
8		Pont-y-Pant	..	..			..	..	..	..	..	..	..	
12¼		Bettws-y-Coed ⊕	arr.	....			....	....	12 5	2 0	2 40	3 0	3 5	
			dep.	..	11 0	11 55	..	..	1 35	3 10	3 31	3 23	3 22	..
16		Llanrwst & Trefriw ⊕	arr.	....	11 10	12 5	....	....	1 45	3 20	3 44	3 33	3 32	Runs on Tal-y-Cafn Sale Days only.
			dep.	..	11 55	1 30	..	1 23	2 10	4 28	3 55	4 30	4 32	
16¾		Tan Lan Siding		....	....	....	....	....	....	....	....	....	SUSPENDED	
		Cae Coch Siding	arr.	..	12 0	..	..	1 28	2 15	..	..	..		
			dep.	....	12 10	....	....	1 37	2 25	....	....	....		
18¼		Abbey Siding	..	..	..	..	..	..	..	..	..	..		
19¼		Dolgarrog	arr.	....	....	....	....	....	2 35	4 38	4 5	4 40		
			dep.	..	..	..	..	..	2 45	4 45	4 15	4 50		
22¼		Tal-y-Cafn and Eglwysbach ⊕	arr.	....	12*25	....	....	....	2 55	4 55	4 25	....	4 52	
			dep.	..	12*37	1*51	..	1*52	3 5	5 5	4 35	5* 0	5 9	5 50
25¾		Glan Conway	arr.	....	....	....	....	X	X	....	....	....	....	....
			dep.	..	..	..	..	..	..	..	..	..	..	..
27¼	329	LLANDUDNO JN. ⊕	arr.	....	12 52	2 6	....	2 9	3 29	5 20	4 49	5 15	5 22	6 5

WEEKDAYS.

Miles	For continuation of trains from junctions, see page			18	19	20	21	23	24	25	27	28	29	31
				Freight.	Freight.		Freight. Commences July 3.	Freight. SUSPENDED commencing July 3.	Freight. Commences July 3.		Freight. SUSPENDED Commencing July 3.	Freight. SUSPENDED commencing July 8.		Light Engine
					Q						SX	SO		Q SX
				a.m.	a.m.		a.m.	a.m.	a.m.		a.m.	a.m.		p.m.
0		LLANDUDNO JN. ⊕	dep.	5 20	....	....	5 35	6 50	8 12	....	11 7	11 7	....	2 48
1½		Glan Conway	arr.	..	..	..	5 40	6 55	..	..	11 12	11 12	..	..
			dep.	....	....	....	5 50	7 5	....	....	11 22	11 22	....	....
5		Tal-y-Cafn and Eglwysbach .. .. ⊕	arr.	..	..	..	6 0	7 15	8 27	..	11 32	11 32	..	3 3
			dep.	5*35	....	....	6 14	7 25	8 40	....	11 58	11 58	....	....
8		Dolgarrog	arr.	Commences July 3.	..	..	6 24	7 35	..	..	12 8	12 8	..	To shunt.
			dep.		....	....	6 34	7 45	....	....	12 18	12 18	....	
		Cae Coch Siding	arr.		..	..	..	See	8 55	..	V	V	..	
			dep.		....	....	....	note	9 5	....	....	....	....	....
10½		Tan Lan Siding	..		..	..	..	..	..	..	..	..	..	..
11¼		Llanrwst & Trefriw ⊕	arr.		....	....	6 44	7 55	9 12	....	12 28	12 28	....	Commences July 3.
			dep.	5*50	..	..	7 40	9 10	10 15	..	1 15	..	..	
15		Bettws-y-Coed ⊕	arr.	....	....	....	7 50	9 20	10 25	....	1 25	....	....	
			dep.	6* 0	..	..	8 55	10 30	..	..	1 54	..	..	
19¼		Pont-y-Pant		....	....	....	....	V	....	....	....	....	....	
20¾		Dolwyddelen .. .. ⊕	arr.	6*25	..	..	9 20	10 50	..	..	2 19	..	..	
			dep.	6*40	....	....	9 40	11 5	....	....	2 42	....	....	....
22½		Roman Bridge	..	..	..	..	..	V	..	..	..	..	..	..
		Greaves' & Oakley's Sidings	....	....	8 42	....	....	....	....	....	....	....	....	....
27¼		BLAENAU FESTINIOG ⊕	arr.	7 0	8 47	..	10 0	11 25	..	..	3 2	..	..	..

6—**X**—Stops at Glan Conway when required for tranship purposes.

8—**X**—Stops at Roman Bridge and Glan Conway when required for tranship purposes.

23—Depart Bettws-y-Coed 10.35 a.m. (SO), Dolwyddelen arr. 10.55, dep. 11.10, Roman Bridge Blaenau Festiniog arr. 11.30.

CREWE, APRIL, 1939. **S. E. PARKHOUSE, Divisional Superintendent of Operat**

151. Betws y Coed. 9th August 1960. The daily freight working, in the hands of Ivatt Class 2T 2-6-2T No.**41228**, prepares for the climb ahead on its way to Blaenau. Leaving Betws at 10.20am, twenty minutes was allowed for the $4^1/_4$ miles to Dolwyddelan where refuge was sought whilst the 10.50am passenger to Llandudno crossed. Arrival in Blaenau was scheduled for 11.15am, followed by a trip working to Greaves Siding as and when required. *Derek Cross.*

British Railways Working Time Table. June 14th to September 19th 1954.

WEEKDAYS — LLANDUDNO JN. TO BLAENAU F.N. — WEEKDAYS

DOWN

Mileage M	C	Station		B	B	B	B	B	B	B	B	B	B	B B B	B	B	B
								10.35 am from Llandudno		2.0 pm from Llandudno					7.55 pm from Llandudno	10.50 pm from Llandudno	10.50 pm from Llandudno
						SO	SX		SX				SX SO		ThO	SO
0	0	LLANDUDNO JN. ... dep	1	am 4 55	am 5 40	am 7 55	am 10 53	am 10 53	PM 12 30	2 16	3 5	PM 3 52	PM 4 48 4 48 6 0	8 10	PM 11 2	PM 11 2
1	31	Glan Conway	2				10a58	10a58	12a35	2a21	3a10	3a57	4a53 4a53 6a 5	8a15		
4	78	Tal-y-Cafn and E. ... arr	3	5 6	5 51	8X 8	11 4	11 4	12 41	2X27	3X16	4X 3	4X59 4 59 6 11	8 21	11X13	11X13
		... dep		5 8	5 52	8 15	11 5	11 5	12 42	2 28	3 20	4 4	5 0 5 0 6 12	8 22	11 16	11 16
8	3	Dolgarrog	4	5 D15	6aD0	8a23	11 12	11 12	12 49	2 35	3 27	4 11	5X14 5 7 6 19	8 30		
11	9	Llanrwst and Trefriw ... arr	5	5 22	6 7	8 30	11 19	11 19	12X56	2X42	3X34	4X18	5X14 5X14 6X26	8X38	11 29	11 29
		... dep		5 33	6 9	8 34	11 21	11 21	12 57	2 43	3 35	4 19	5 18 5 18 6 29	8 40	11 30	11 30
14	76	Betws-y-Coed ... arr	6	5 33	6 16	8 41	11X28	11X28	1X4	2 50	3X42	4 26	5 25 5 25 6 36	8 47	11 37	11 37
		... dep		5 36	6 19	8 46	11 31	11 31	1 8		3 43	4a42	5 38 6 39	8 50		11 40
19	22	Pont-y-pant	10	V	6a32	8a59	11a44	11 44	1a21		3a56		5a51 6a52	9a 3		
20	55	Dolwyddelen ... arr	11	5 53	6 36	9X3	11 48	11 48	1X25		4 0	4X46	5X55 6X56	9 7		11 57
		... dep		5 55	6 38	9 7	11 50	11 50	1 30		4 1	4 51	6 0 6 58	9 10		11 59
22	40	Roman Bridge	13	6Dc2	6c45	9c14	11c57	11c57	1c37		4c10	4c59	6c 7 7c 6	9c17		
27	19	BLAENAU F. N. ... arr	14	6 14	6 57	9 26	12 9	12 9	1 49		4 22	5 11	6 19 7 18	9 29		12 16

WEEKDAYS — BLAENAU F.N. TO LLANDUDNO JN. — WEEKDAYS — SUNDAYS

UP

Mileage M	C	Station		B To Llandudno	B To Llandudno Jn. SX,SO	B To Llandudno Jn. SX,SO	B To Llandudno Jn. SX,SO	B To Llandudno	B To Llandudno	B To Llandudno	B To Llandudno	B To Llandudno	B To Llandudno	B	C ECS	C ECS
								SX	SX		SX	SO		ThO		
0	0	B'LAENAU F. N. ... dep	1	am 7 5	am 8 45	am 10 54	PM 12 27	PM 2 18	PM	PM 4 30	5 39	PM 6 36	PM 7 51	PM 10 15	am 12;37
4	59	Roman Bridge	2	7c19	8c59	11c 8	12c41	2c32		4c44	5c53	6c50	8c 5	10c29	
6	44	Dolwyddelen ... arr	3	7 24	9X4	11 13	12X46	2 37		4X49	5X58	6X55	8 10	10 34	12 53
		... dep	4	7 25	9 5	11 14	12 47	2 38		4 50	5 59	7 0	8 11	10 35	
7	77	Font-y-pant	5	7a29	9a 9	11a18	12a51	2a42		4a54		7a 4	8a15	10a39	
12	23	Betws-y-Coed ... arr	6	7 40	9X29	11X29	1X2	2 53		5 5	6 14	7 16	8 26	10 50	1* 8
		... dep	7	7 44	9 22	11 33	1 6	2 56	4 9	5 9	6 17	7 10 7 19	8 28	10 54	11;55	1*11
16	10	Llanrwst and Trefriw ... arr	8	7X51	9 29	11 40	1 13	3 3	4X16	5X16	6X24	7 17 7 26	8X36	11 1	
		... dep	9	7 52	9 30	11 41	1 14	3 4	4 20	5 17	6 29	7 18 7 27	8 40	11 2	12 2	1 10
19	16	Dolgarrog	10	7 59	9 37	11 46	1 28	3 11	4 28	5 25	6 37	7 27 7 36	8 48	11X15	
22	21	Tal-y-Cafn and E. ... arr	11	8X 7	9X44	11 56	1 28	3X18	4 35	5 33	6 44	7 34 7 43	8 55	11 16	12 12	1 30
		... dep	12	8 10	9 45	11 57	1 29	3 19	4 36	5 33	6 45	7 35 7 44	8 56	11 16	
25	68	Glan Conway	13	8a17	9a52	12a 4	1a36	3a26	4a43	5 40	6 52	7 42 7 51	9 3		
27	19	LLANDUDNO JN. ... arr	14	8 21	9 56	12 8	1 40	3 30	4 47	5 44	6 56	7 47 7 56	9 7	11 25	12;22	1;40

H110 WEEKDAYS — LLANDUDNO JUNCTION AND BLAENAU F.N.

DOWN

Mileage M	C	Station		K 28 Q	K am
0	0	LLANDUDNO JN. dep		am 6 30	
1	48	Glan Conway ... arr		6 35	
		... dep		6 45	
5	16	Tal-y-Cafn and Eglwybach ... arr		6 55	
		... dep		7 16	
8	20	Dolgarrog ... arr		7 26	
		... dep		7 36	
11	18	Llanrwst and Trefriw ... arr		7X46	
		... dep		8 47	
15	0	Betws-y-Coed ... arr		8X57	
		... dep		9 45	
19	38	Pontypant			
20	71	Dolwyddelen ... arr		10 5	
		... dep		10 25	
22	60	Roman Bridge			
26	46	Greave's Siding			11 40
27	19	BLAENAU F.N. ... arr		10 45	11 45

UP

Mileage M	C	Station		K 28 Q	K PM
0	0	BLAENAU F.N. ... dep		am 11 20	12 50
0	53	Greave's Siding		11 25	
4	39	Roman Bridge			
6	28	Dolwyddelen ... arr			1X10
		... dep			1 44
7	61	Pontypant			
12	19	Betws-y-Coed ... arr			2 4
		... dep			2 25
16	1	Llanrwst and Trefriw ... arr			2X35
		... dep			3 35
18	79	Dolgarrog ... arr			3 46
		... dep			3 52
22	3	Tal-y-Cafn and Eglwybach ... arr			4X2
		... dep			4 7
25	51	Glan Conway ... arr			
		... dep			
27	19	LLANDUDNO JN. arr			4 22

152. Blaenau Ffestiniog. [Above]. This 2 feet gauge wagon is thought to be of a type built by the LNWR at Earlestown to ease transhipment of slate from the quarries around Blaenau to Deganwy, where a wharf had been specially built by the company to deal with the traffic. Loaded wagons were transferred onto other specially built standard gauge wagons, which had transversely fixed small section rails, -enabling three narrow gauge vehicles to be carried. An example of this can be seen in plate 3.

E.R.W. Higgs.

153. Blaenau Ffestiniog. 5th July 1952. The slate wharfs in Blaenau goods yard were still much in use as this view shows, with stacks of graded slates awaiting transportation behind the loaded narrow gauge wagons. *J.J. Davis.*

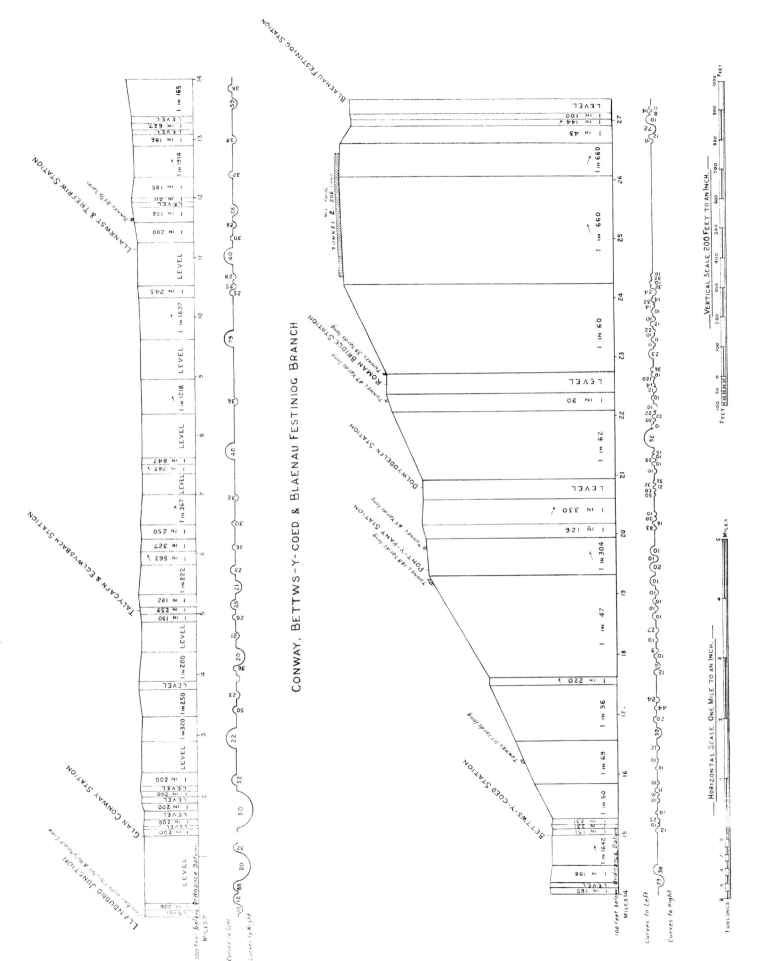

CONWAY, BETTWS-Y-COED & BLAENAU FESTINIOG BRANCH.

CONWAY, BETTWS-Y-COED & BLAENAU FESTINIOG BRANCH

VERTICAL SCALE 200 FEET TO AN INCH.

HORIZONTAL SCALE, ONE MILE TO AN INCH.

The Conwy Valley line continues to be an attraction for the many visitors to the area although it is now little more than a very basic railway with minimal operating or staff requirements. This has not however diminished the variety and nature of either the motive power or rolling stock that occasionally traverses the route. These last few pages contain photographs from the camera of **Larry Goddard**.

154. 6th September 1990. [Upper]. On its periodical visit to the area, the Schering Agriculture Chesterton Junction, Cambridge Weedkilling Train - to give its full title - is seen working north between Tal-y-Cafn and Glan Conwy. The two Class 20 locomotives, **20902** *Lorna*, and **20905** *Iona*, are owned by Hunslet Barclay Ltd., and painted in a distinctive two-tone grey livery with red lettering. The carriages are converted Mk.I stock in bright green livery and consist of Spray (next to tank wagons), Generator and stores, Staff and workshop, and Dormitory vehicles. Note the extensive repairs to the river bank, a reminder of the constant threat to the railway.

155. Tal-y-Cafn, 25th July 1986. [Centre]. These Class 142 'Pacer' units were relatively new when **142038** seen leaving Tal-y-Cafn with the 12.15pm Llandudno to Blaenau Ffestiniog service. The units were subsequently barred from the line.

156. Llanrwst. 5th August 1989. [Lower]. The years of rationalization seem far away as Chester unit **CH373** pulls away from the new station with the 12.00pm Blaenau Ffestiniog to Llandudno working. It was thought that this location would serve the town better than the original and duly opened on 29th July.

157. Between Betws y Coed and Llanrwst. 4th June 1987. [upper]. One of the most picturesque locations on the line is the river crossing south of Llanrwst. The Conwy occasionally bursts its banks in the upper parts of the valley, sometimes causing damage to the railway. For the moment however, the scene is tranquil as Class 31 No.**31201** heads north to Llandudno Junction with a freight working from Maentwrog Road.   *Larry Goddard.*

*1*58. Blaenau Ffestiniog, 26th May 1986.On the first day of "Sprinter" operation, Class 150/1 units, **150102** and **150112** emerge from Ffestiniog Tunnel with the 14.40 service from Llandudno. Their visits to the line were comparatively short lived due to the excessive noise generated by wheel flange contact. The Department of the Environment consequently barred the class from working the line and so "Heritage" DMU's returned, to the route on 29th June 1987.

Larry Goddard.

159. Blaenau Ffestiniog. August 1963. [Upper] It would be incorrect to say that the view was magnificent, but the presence of the huge deposits of slate appears impressive to say the least. The railway is in decline but the yard is still active, with a goodly collection of narrow gauge slate wagons to the far right. There is also a solitary narrow gauge track along the transhipment wharf although it is perhaps difficult to imagine what purpose it serves. The line to the left forms the connection with the former G.W. route to Trawsfynydd although at the time of the photograph it had yet to be officially opened for traffic.

160. Blaenau Ffestiniog. 7th October 1990. [Lower]. The interchange at Blaenau opened in 1982 to give a much needed boost to the Conwy Valley line. The new station on the site of the former G.W.R. Central terminus, brought both the British Rail and the Festiniog Railway into the town once more. The canopy for passengers on the narrow gauge is the latest in a number of improvements which presumably will culminate in tracks on both sides of the island platform. On this occasion we see a three-car DMU and a Class 31, with the Trawsfynydd freight, stabled in the loop, a situation caused by high river levels near Betws y Coed which effectively trapped the stock. Former Penrhyn Railway 0-4-0 *Linda* was awaiting departure for Porthmadog with the F.R. train.